1st EDITION

Perspectives on Diseases and Disorders

Celiac Disease

Jacqueline Langwith

Book Editor

PERSPECTIVES
On Diseases & Disorders

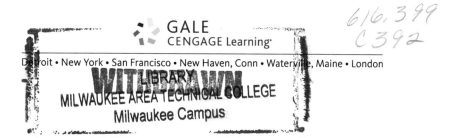

GALE
CENGAGE Learning·

Detroit • New York • San Francisco • New Haven, Conn • Waterville, Maine • London

Elizabeth Des Chenes, *Director, Publishing Solutions*

For more information, contact:
Greenhaven Press
27500 Drake Rd.
Farmington Hills, MI 48331-3535
Or you can visit our Internet site at gale.cengage.com

For product information and technology assistance, contact us at

Gale Customer Support, 1-800-877-4253
For permission to use material from this text or product, submit all requests online at
www.cengage.com/permissions

Further permissions questions can be e-mailed to permissionrequest@cengage.com

Articles in Greenhaven Press anthologies are often edited for length to meet page requirements. In addition, original titles of these works are changed to clearly present the main thesis and to explicitly indicate the author's opinion. Every effort is made to ensure that Greenhaven Press accurately reflects the original intent of the authors. Every effort has been made to trace the owners of copyrighted material.

Cover image © ISM/Phototake. All rights reserved.

LIBRARY OF CONGRESS CATALOGING-IN-PUBLICATION DATA

Celiac disease / Jacqueline Langwith, book editor.
   p. cm. -- (Perspectives on diseases and disorders)
  Summary: "Celiac Disease: Each volume in this timely series provides essential information on a disease or disorder (symptoms, causes, treatments, cures, etc.); presents the controversies surrounding causes, alternative treatments, and other issues"-- Provided by publisher.
  Includes bibliographical references and index.
  ISBN 978-0-7377-5772-9 (hardback)
  1. Celiac disease--Juvenile literature. I. Langwith, Jacqueline.
  RC862.C44C423 2012
  616.3'99--dc23
                                          2012006901

Printed in the United States of America
1 2 3 4 5 6 7 16 15 14 13 12

CONTENTS

CHAPTER 2   Controversies Concerning Celiac Disease

"Medicine, to produce health, has to examine disease."
—Plutarch

Independent research on a health issue is often the first step to complement discussions with a physician. But locating accurate, well-organized, understandable medical information can be a challenge. A simple Internet search on terms such as "cancer" or "diabetes," for example, returns an intimidating number of results. Sifting through the results can be daunting, particularly when some of the information is inconsistent or even contradictory. The Greenhaven Press series Perspectives on Diseases and Disorders offers a solution to the often overwhelming nature of researching diseases and disorders.

From the clinical to the personal, titles in the Perspectives on Diseases and Disorders series provide students and other researchers with authoritative, accessible information in unique anthologies that include basic information about the disease or disorder, controversial aspects of diagnosis and treatment, and first-person accounts of those impacted by the disease. The result is a well-rounded combination of primary and secondary sources that, together, provide the reader with a better understanding of the disease or disorder.

Each volume in Perspectives on Diseases and Disorders explores a particular disease or disorder in detail. Material for each volume is carefully selected from a wide range of sources, including encyclopedias, journals, newspapers, nonfiction books, speeches, government documents, pamphlets, organization newsletters, and position papers. Articles in the first chapter provide an authoritative, up-to-date overview that covers symptoms, causes and effects, treatments, cures, and medical advances. The second chapter presents a substantial number of opposing viewpoints on controversial treatments and other current debates relating to the volume topic. The third chapter offers a variety of personal perspectives on the disease or disorder. Patients, doctors, caregivers, and loved ones represent just some of the voices found in this narrative chapter.

Each Perspectives on Diseases and Disorders volume also includes:

- An **annotated table of contents** that provides a brief summary of each article in the volume.
- An **introduction** specific to the volume topic.
- Full-color **charts and graphs** to illustrate key points, concepts, and theories.
- Full-color **photos** that show aspects of the disease or disorder and enhance textual material.
- **"Fast Facts"** that highlight pertinent additional statistics and surprising points.
- A **glossary** providing users with definitions of important terms.
- A **chronology** of important dates relating to the disease or disorder.
- An annotated list of **organizations to contact** for students and other readers seeking additional information.
- A **bibliography** of additional books and periodicals for further research.
- A detailed **subject index** that allows readers to quickly find the information they need.

Whether a student researching a disorder, a patient recently diagnosed with a disease, or an individual who simply wants to learn more about a particular disease or disorder, a reader who turns to Perspectives on Diseases and Disorders will find a wealth of information in each volume that offers not only basic information, but also vigorous debate from multiple perspectives.

INTRODUCTION

Millions of US couples struggle with the heartbreak of infertility. Infertility is defined as the biological inability of a woman or man to contribute to conception; many experts explain infertility as not being able to get pregnant after at least one year of trying. Women who do get pregnant but then have repeated miscarriages are also said to be infertile. According to the American Fertility Association (AFA), one out of every eight couples in the United States is infertile. Most of these couples will discover the reason for their infertility, whether it be a male or a female reproductive issue; however, says the AFA, 20 percent of these couples will be diagnosed with unexplained infertility. In recent years, researchers have found an association between celiac disease and reproductive problems that may provide the cause of some women's unexplained infertility.

A number of studies in recent decades have associated celiac disease with reproductive problems. Studies going back at least ten years in several different countries have compared the prevalence of reproductive disorders in women and men who have celiac disease with those who do not. Two different Italian studies, conducted in 1996 and 2008, found that women with celiac disease were significantly more likely to suffer miscarriages than women without celiac disease. In a study conducted in Iran in 2006 and 2007, it was found that infertile couples are more likely to test positive for celiac disease antibodies than fertile couples, and the prevalence rate of celiac disease in infertile patients was more than twice the prevalence rate in fertile couples. Other studies have shown that women with celiac disease have their periods later than other women but start menopause earlier, and they are more likely to have irregular menstrual cycles.

Although these studies suggest an association between celiac disease and reproductive issues in women, most experts say that more studies are needed before researchers can say conclusively that celiac disease causes infertility.

Researchers have found a connection between reproductive disorders and celiac disease that may explain some women's infertility. (© **Bubbles Photolibrary/Alamy**)

Sheila Crowe, a professor in the Department of Gastroenterology and Hepatology in the School of Medicine at the University of Virginia, explained the issue to readers of the *New York Times Health Consults* blog on February 3, 2010. According to Crowe, "There are many causes of infertility, miscarriages, and small babies besides unrecognized celiac disease, and some studies have failed to show that the risks of these problems are actually increased by untreated celiac disease." Crowe went on to say that "larger and better-devised studies are needed," but that in her own clinical experience, "infertility and smaller or preterm babies are more common in women with untreated celiac disease than [in] those without."[1]

Crowe is not the only person who does not need convincing that celiac disease is associated with infertility. Sunshine is a thirty-something blogger who was told she had unexplained infertility. In March 2011, on the website IVFconnections.com, Sunshine shared the story of her struggles with infertility. During a five-year period, Sunshine endured more than ten failed in vitro fertilization (IVF) procedures, several miscarriages—including one that tragically occurred at 20 weeks—and multiple failed surrogate and donor arrangements. As she explains in her story, "We're heartbroken and just downright broken after 10 IVFs, no baby, and absolutely NO clue what our problem is. . . . How can I fight an enemy we aren't aware of?" Then, according to Sunshine, she received a phone call from her sister that changed her life. Her sister had seen Elisabeth Hasselbeck promoting her book about celiac disease on the TV show *Dr. Oz* and thought that celiac disease could explain many of Sunshine's health issues, including her infertility. As it turned out, her sister was right. After testing positive for celiac disease, Sunshine felt she finally had an enemy she could fight. As she explained, "I had my infertility diagnosis. If I wasn't being properly nourished, my eggs were probably compromised. And of course, how could my body grow a fetus then?" Sunshine's doctor advised her to remove all gluten-containing foods from her diet and then start trying to conceive again. Since she did not want to risk the tragedy of another twenty-week miscarriage, Sunshine decided to use a carrier to nurture the healthy embryos created by her and her husband. Finally, Sunshine's infertility struggles were over, and she became the mother of twins. In her story, Sunshine expresses frustration that none of her doctors thought to check for celiac disease as a factor in her infertility. As she writes, "I hope my story helps even just one person out—I went through five years and 11 IVFs for no reason. I am infuriated that not one GI [gastrointestinal specialist] or RE [reproductive endocrinologist] asked me just one simple question, or took just one more vial of blood from the hundreds I had done over the years."[2]

Sunshine's experience demonstrates the difficulties celiac disease poses to both patients and doctors. It is a disease that most people associate with the digestive system; however, it may affect other systems, including the skin, the skeletal system, the neurological system, and the reproductive system. It is also associated with diabetes, osteoporosis, and several other disorders. In *Perspectives on Diseases and Disorders: Celiac Disease*, the contributors provide the latest science, discuss the current controversies, and convey the personal experiences associated with this challenging and frequently undiagnosed disease.

Notes

1. Sheila Crowe, "Can Foods Contribute to Infertility?," *New York Times Health Consults* (blog), February 3, 2010. http://consults.blogs.nytimes.com/2010/02/03/can -foods-contribute-to-infertility.
2. Sunshine, "Sunshine's Story: A 23-Year Medical Mystery Finally Solved," IVF Connections, March 16, 2011. www.ivfconnections.com/forums/content.php/760 -Sunshines-Story-A-23-Year-Medical-Mystery-Finally -Solved/view/5.

CHAPTER 1

Understanding Celiac Disease

An Overview of Celiac Disease

National Institute of Diabetes and Digestive and Kidney Diseases

Celiac disease is an autoimmune disorder of the digestive system that affects more than 2 million people in the United States, according to the National Institute of Diabetes and Digestive and Kidney Diseases (NIDDK). With celiac disease, gluten, a protein found in wheat, barley, and rye, causes an immune response that damages or destroys the villi, tiny sacs in the lining of the small intestine. People with celiac disease cannot properly absorb nutrients and become sick from the immune response. According to the NIDDK, the only treatment for celiac disease is to avoid gluten-containing foods and products.

The NIDDK is one of twenty-seven institutes and centers of the National Institutes of Health. The NIDDK conducts and supports basic and clinical research on many of the most serious diseases affecting public health.

Photo on facing page. People with celiac disease cannot tolerate a specific protein found in wheat, rye, barley, and other grains. (© Hannah Gal/ Photo Researchers, Inc.)

SOURCE: National Institute of Diabetes and Digestive and Kidney Diseases, "Celiac Disease," National Digestive Diseases Information Clearinghouse. http://digestive.niddk.nih.gov, September 2008.

Celiac disease is a digestive disease that damages the small intestine and interferes with absorption of nutrients from food. People who have celiac disease cannot tolerate gluten, a protein in wheat, rye, and barley. Gluten is found mainly in foods but may also be found in everyday products such as medicines, vitamins, and lip balms.

When people with celiac disease eat foods or use products containing gluten, their immune system responds by damaging or destroying villi—the tiny, fingerlike protrusions lining the small intestine. Villi normally allow nutrients from food to be absorbed through the walls of the small intestine into the bloodstream. Without healthy villi, a person becomes malnourished, no matter how much food one eats.

Celiac disease is both a disease of malabsorption—meaning nutrients are not absorbed properly—and an abnormal immune reaction to gluten. Celiac disease is also known as celiac sprue, nontropical sprue, and gluten-sensitive enteropathy. Celiac disease is genetic, meaning it runs in families. Sometimes the disease is triggered—or becomes active for the first time—after surgery, pregnancy, childbirth, viral infection, or severe emotional stress.

Celiac Disease Symptoms

Symptoms of celiac disease vary from person to person. Symptoms may occur in the digestive system or in other parts of the body. Digestive symptoms are more common in infants and young children and may include

- abdominal bloating and pain
- chronic diarrhea
- vomiting
- constipation
- pale, foul-smelling, or fatty stool
- weight loss

Villi in the Small Intestine

Villi on the lining of the small intestine help absorb nutrients. For those who have celiac disease, gluten causes damage to the villi.

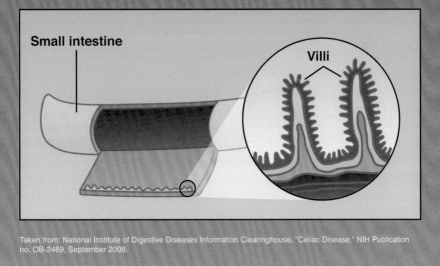

Taken from: National Institute of Digestive Diseases Information Clearinghouse, "Celiac Disease," NIH Publication no. OB-2469, September 2008.

Irritability is another common symptom in children. Malabsorption of nutrients during the years when nutrition is critical to a child's normal growth and development can result in other problems such as failure to thrive in infants, delayed growth and short stature, delayed puberty, and dental enamel defects of the permanent teeth.

Adults are less likely to have digestive symptoms and may instead have one or more of the following:

- unexplained iron-deficiency anemia
- fatigue
- bone or joint pain
- arthritis
- bone loss or osteoporosis
- depression or anxiety
- tingling numbness in the hands and feet
- seizures
- missed menstrual periods

- infertility or recurrent miscarriage
- canker sores inside the mouth
- an itchy skin rash called dermatitis herpetiformis

People with celiac disease may have no symptoms but can still develop complications of the disease over time. Long-term complications include malnutrition—which can lead to anemia, osteoporosis, and miscarriage, among other problems—liver diseases, and cancers of the intestine.

Researchers are studying the reasons celiac disease affects people differently. The length of time a person was breastfed, the age a person started eating gluten-containing foods, and the amount of gluten-containing foods one eats are three factors thought to play a role in when and how celiac disease appears. Some studies have shown, for example, that the longer a person was breast-fed, the later the symptoms of celiac disease appear.

Symptoms also vary depending on a person's age and the degree of damage to the small intestine. Many adults have the disease for a decade or more before they are di-agnosed. The longer a person goes undiagnosed and un-treated, the greater the chance of developing long-term complications.

Genetics and Links to Other Diseases

People with celiac disease tend to have other diseases in which the immune system attacks the body's healthy cells and tissues. The connection between celiac disease and these diseases may be genetic. They include

- type 1 diabetes
- autoimmune thyroid disease
- autoimmune liver disease
- rheumatoid arthritis
- Addison's disease, a condition in which the glands that produce critical hormones are damaged
- Sjögren's syndrome, a condition in which the glands that produce tears and saliva are destroyed

Celiac disease affects people in all parts of the world. Originally thought to be a rare childhood syndrome, celiac disease is now known to be a common genetic disorder. More than 2 million people in the United States have the disease, or about 1 in 133 people. Among people who have a first-degree relative—a parent, sibling, or child—diagnosed with celiac disease, as many as 1 in 22 people may have the disease.

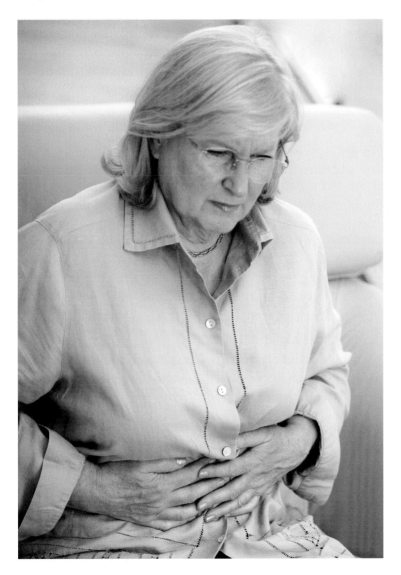

Indications of celiac disease may include various symptoms, such as abdominal bloating and pain. Many adults go for years before the disease is diagnosed. (© BSIP/ Photo Researchers, Inc.)

Celiac disease is also more common among people with other genetic disorders, including Down syndrome and Turner syndrome, a condition that affects girls' development.

Diagnosing Celiac Disease

Recognizing celiac disease can be difficult because some of its symptoms are similar to those of other diseases. Celiac disease can be confused with irritable bowel syndrome, iron-deficiency anemia caused by menstrual blood loss, inflammatory bowel disease, diverticulitis, intestinal infections, and chronic fatigue syndrome. As a result, celiac disease has long been underdiagnosed or misdiagnosed. As doctors become more aware of the many varied symptoms of the disease and reliable blood tests become more available, diagnosis rates are increasing.

People with celiac disease have higher than normal levels of certain autoantibodies—proteins that react against the body's own cells or tissues—in their blood. To diagnose celiac disease, doctors will test blood for high levels of anti-tissue transglutaminase antibodies (tTGA) or anti-endomysium antibodies (EMA). If test results are negative but celiac disease is still suspected, additional blood tests may be needed.

Before being tested, one should continue to eat a diet that includes foods with gluten, such as breads and pastas. If a person stops eating foods with gluten before being tested, the results may be negative for celiac disease even if the disease is present.

If blood tests and symptoms suggest celiac disease, a biopsy of the small intestine is performed to confirm the diagnosis. During the biopsy, the doctor removes tiny pieces of tissue from the small intestine to check for damage to the villi. To obtain the tissue sample, the doctor eases a long, thin tube called an endoscope through the patient's mouth

FAST FACT

The number of people with celiac disease in the United States would fill forty-four hundred Boeing 747 airliners, according to the University of Chicago Celiac Disease Center.

and stomach into the small intestine. The doctor then takes the samples using instruments passed through the endoscope.

Dermatitis herpetiformis (DH) is an intensely itchy, blistering skin rash that affects 15 to 25 percent of people with celiac disease. The rash usually occurs on the elbows, knees, and buttocks. Most people with DH have no digestive symptoms of celiac disease.

DH is diagnosed through blood tests and a skin biopsy. If the antibody tests are positive and the skin biopsy has the typical findings of DH, patients do not need to have an intestinal biopsy. Both the skin disease and the intestinal disease respond to a gluten-free diet and recur if gluten is added back into the diet. The rash symptoms can be controlled with antibiotics such as dapsone. Because dapsone does not treat the intestinal condition, people with DH must maintain a gluten-free diet.

Screening for celiac disease means testing for the presence of autoantibodies in the blood in people without symptoms. Americans are not routinely screened for celiac disease. However, because celiac disease is hereditary, family members of a person with the disease may wish to be tested. Four to 12 percent of an affected person's first-degree relatives will also have the disease.

Treating Celiac Disease: The Gluten-Free Diet

The only treatment for celiac disease is a gluten-free diet. Doctors may ask a newly diagnosed person to work with a dietitian on a gluten-free diet plan. A dietitian is a health care professional who specializes in food and nutrition. Someone with celiac disease can learn from a dietitian how to read ingredient lists and identify foods that contain gluten in order to make informed decisions at the grocery store and when eating out.

For most people, following this diet will stop symptoms, heal existing intestinal damage, and prevent further damage. Improvement begins within days of starting the diet. The small intestine usually heals in 3 to 6 months in children but may take several years in adults. A healed intestine means a person now has villi that can absorb nutrients from food into the bloodstream.

To stay well, people with celiac disease must avoid gluten for the rest of their lives. Eating even a small amount of gluten can damage the small intestine. The damage will occur in anyone with the disease, including people without noticeable symptoms. Depending on a person's age at diagnosis, some problems will not improve, such as short stature and dental enamel defects.

Some people with celiac disease show no improvement on the gluten-free diet. The most common reason for poor response to the diet is that small amounts of gluten are still being consumed. Hidden sources of gluten include additives such as modified food starch, preservatives, and stabilizers made with wheat. And because many corn and rice products are produced in factories that also manufacture wheat products, they can be contaminated with wheat gluten.

Rarely, the intestinal injury will continue despite a strictly gluten-free diet. People with this condition, known as refractory celiac disease, have severely damaged intestines that cannot heal. Because their intestines are not absorbing enough nutrients, they may need to receive nutrients directly into their bloodstream through a vein, or intravenously. Researchers are evaluating drug treatments for refractory celiac disease.

A gluten-free diet means not eating foods that contain wheat, rye, and barley. The foods and products made from these grains should also be avoided. In other words, a person with celiac disease should not eat most grain, pasta, cereal, and many processed foods.

Despite these restrictions, people with celiac disease can eat a well-balanced diet with a variety of foods. They can use potato, rice, soy, amaranth, quinoa, buckwheat, or bean flour instead of wheat flour. They can buy gluten-free bread, pasta, and other products from stores that carry organic foods, or order products from special food companies. Gluten-free products are increasingly available from mainstream stores.

"Plain" meat, fish, rice, fruits, and vegetables do not contain gluten, so people with celiac disease can freely eat these foods. In the past, people with celiac disease were advised not to eat oats. New evidence suggests that most people can safely eat small amounts of oats, as long as the oats are not contaminated with wheat gluten during processing. People with celiac disease should work closely with their health care team when deciding whether to include oats in their diet. . . .

A New Approach to Eating

The gluten-free diet requires a completely new approach to eating. Newly diagnosed people and their families may find support groups helpful as they learn to adjust to a new way of life. People with celiac disease must be cautious about what they buy for lunch at school or work, what they purchase at the grocery store, what they eat at restaurants or parties, and what they grab for a snack. Eating out can be a challenge. When in doubt about a menu item, a person with celiac disease should ask the waiter or chef about ingredients and preparation or if a gluten-free menu is available.

Gluten is also used in some medications. People with celiac disease should ask a pharmacist if prescribed medications contain wheat. Because gluten is sometimes used as an additive in unexpected products—such as lipstick and play dough—reading product labels is important. If the ingredients are not listed on the label, the manufacturer should provide a list upon request. With practice, screening for gluten becomes second nature.

The Food Allergen Labeling and Consumer Protection Act (FALCPA), which took effect on January 1,

2006, requires food labels to clearly identify wheat and other common food allergens in the list of ingredients. FALCPA also requires the U.S. Food and Drug Administration to develop and finalize rules for the use of the term "gluten-free" on product labels. . . .

New Developments

The National Institute of Diabetes and Digestive and Kidney Diseases conducts and supports research on celiac disease. Researchers are studying new options for diagnosing celiac disease, including capsule endoscopy. In this technique, patients swallow a capsule containing a tiny video camera that records images of the small intestine.

Several drug treatments for celiac disease are under evaluation. Researchers are also studying a combination of enzymes—proteins that aid chemical reactions in the body—that detoxify gluten before it enters the small intestine.

Scientists are also developing educational materials for standardized medical training to raise awareness among health care providers. The hope is that increased understanding and awareness will lead to earlier diagnosis and treatment of celiac disease.

Confirming a Diagnosis of Celiac Disease

Sheila Crowe

According to Sheila Crowe in the following viewpoint, celiac disease is diagnosed by an abnormal result on a biopsy of the small intestine. Blood antibody tests can help to indicate whether a person has celiac disease; however, blood tests have significant rates of false negatives and false positives, so Crowe says confirming a diagnosis of celiac disease always requires an intestinal biopsy. She cautions people against going gluten-free before a celiac diagnosis is confirmed, as this can complicate biopsy results.

Crowe is a professor in the Department of Gastroenterology (stomach and intestinal studies) and Hepatology (liver studies) in the School of Medicine at the University of Virginia.

By definition, a diagnosis of celiac disease requires abnormal microscopic findings in small intestinal biopsy specimens. One exception to this rule occurs when a patient has a skin condition known as dermatitis herpetiformis, in which case a characteristically abnormal skin biopsy result can substitute for checking intestinal biopsies.

Since getting an intestinal biopsy is not necessarily the first test anyone wants to undergo, it is fortunate that several blood tests are helpful during the initial steps of diagnosing celiac disease. These blood tests measure antibodies—usually IgA or IgG [immunoglobulin A or G]—that are made by immune cells to two main proteins.

One protein is an enzyme called tissue transglutaminase, or TTG, that is found in many cells of our body. TTG is released from the damaged intestine during active celiac disease, and antibodies to TTG are found to be elevated in the blood of most patients with untreated celiac disease.

The other protein to which the body's immune system responds abnormally in someone with active celiac disease (and occasionally in some other disorders) is a group of proteins found in gluten called gliadins.

FAST FACT

According to several studies, the average delay in diagnosis for adult patients with celiac disease in North America ranges from four to eleven years.

The TTG IgA Antibody Test

At present, the standard of care based on the National Institutes of Health consensus conference on celiac disease, which was held in June 2004 and recommended in the American Gastroenterological Association position statement on celiac disease published in Dec. 2006, is to check for celiac disease using the TTG IgA antibody test. This test will correctly predict the finding of celiac disease on intestinal biopsies roughly 90 to 95 percent of the time, although some recent studies suggest it is less sensitive than initially thought.

In some cases, the TTG IgA test result can be "false negative"—that is, results come back negative, even though celiac disease is actually present. False negatives can occur for various reasons, but the best known cause is a condition called IgA deficiency that [some] people are born with. This immunodeficiency occurs in about one in 600 healthy individuals but is much more common in those with celiac disease.

To help prevent false negatives, most laboratories will measure the total IgA level at the same time as the TTG IgA level. If you are IgA deficient, then your total IgA level will be very low, and that means there's a very good chance that the TTG IgA test will be inaccurate (falsely low or normal) because you can't make IgA antibodies to TTG or gliadin. In this case, your doctor will need to proceed to intestinal biopsies to confirm the suspicion of celiac disease. Occasionally your doctor may order other blood tests, such as TTG IgG or DGP [deamidated gliadin peptide] IgG, if they are available.

An earlier blood test that detected IgA antibodies to TTG called the antiendomysial antibody, or EMA, test is more expensive and time-consuming to perform than the current automated method of testing for TTG, so EMA testing is rarely done now. Another blood test that measures IgG [antibodies] to TTG is rarely tested for in most laboratories.

Gliadin Tests

The first antibodies to gliadin that were used for celiac disease testing are called antigliadin, or AG, antibodies, which are available in both IgA and IgG forms. Most diagnostic laboratories run AG tests for both types of antibodies.

More recently, researchers found that the body makes IgA and IgG antibodies to a form of gliadin called deamidated gliadin peptide, or DGP. Some laboratories are starting to test for these antibodies, too. These new DGP tests seem to be more accurate than the older generation of AG tests.

In adults, AG antibody tests are no longer recommended, as they are not very likely to correctly predict the findings of intestinal biopsies, with both false negative and false positive results. AG tests are reported to be elevated in quite a few other conditions, including Crohn's disease [an intestinal disorder], small intestinal bacterial overgrowth, food intolerances (including gluten sensitivity without celiac disease) and irritable bowel syndrome. AG tests may even be elevated in healthy individuals.

The DGP antibodies seem to be more accurate than the AG tests, with fewer false positive results than the TTG IgA test. However, at this time, the DGP antibodies are not routinely available for clinical use.

In young children, the TTG test is less sensitive—that is, it is less likely to be positive when celiac disease is actually present—than in adults. Therefore, both AG and TTG antibodies are checked in young children.

Another important point is that all of the information we have discussed above relates to blood antibody tests only. While antibody tests have been developed using saliva and stool, these tests are not sufficiently scientifically validated to be acceptable to the general scientific and medical community at this time. TTG tests are available to consumers for purchase in Canada but they are not approved for use in the United States. . . .

Intestinal Biopsy

Even the best antibody tests have some inaccuracies, including a false negative rate. Because of this, I would like to emphasize that if an individual patient's case points to celiac disease, even if all antibody tests are negative, then the next step should be to undergo an upper G.I. [gastrointestinal] endoscopy [insertion of a fiber-optic scope] to obtain small intestinal biopsy samples. This test is also referred to as an esophagogastroduodenoscopy [scoping of the esophagus, stomach, and duodenum (the first twelve inches of the small intestine)], or EGD.

Factors that would lead me to recommend an endoscopy, even if antibodies were negative, include:

- gastrointestinal symptoms such as weight loss, diarrhea, abdominal pain or discomfort;
- severe premature osteoporosis that is otherwise unexplained; and/or
- abnormal lab tests, such as iron deficiency or an elevated fecal fat.

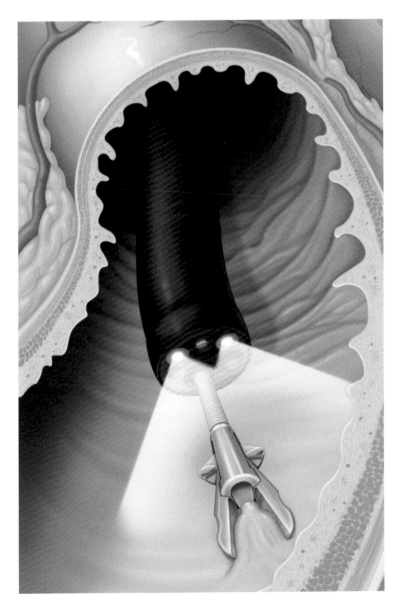

A cutaway view of the small intestine shows a flexible endoscope with biopsy forceps. To confirm a diagnosis of celiac disease, an intestinal biopsy is required. (© Mark Miller/Photo Researchers, Inc.)

The indication for doing an endoscopy with intestinal biopsies would be even greater if combined with a documented family history of celiac disease or a personal history of autoimmune diseases that are highly associated with celiac disease, such as autoimmune thyroid diseases or juvenile diabetes.

The Limits of Testing

Bear in mind that no test is perfect, even the intestinal biopsy, the so-called gold standard of diagnosing celiac disease. Just like with the blood antibody tests, false positive and false negative biopsy results can occur, although the rates of false positives or negatives are very low when experts are involved. Some of these errors arise when insufficient samples are taken: a minimum of four to six biopsy samples are recommended to be taken from the first part of the small intestine (the duodenal bulb) as well as from other parts of the duodenum and jejunum [the section of small intestine after the duodenum], especially from areas where the intestinal lining appears abnormal. Inaccurate results can also occur when specimens are poorly prepared, or when a less experienced pathologist interprets the biopsy sample.

Occasionally, celiac disease is only found further down the small bowel, beyond the reach of the standard upper G.I. endoscope and biopsy forceps. In that case, capsule endoscopy can be used to identify abnormal intestinal lining, and a longer endoscope called an enteroscope may be used to get biopsy samples from these areas, if possible. Another approach is to take biopsies from the end of the small bowel (the ileum) during a colonoscopy. Having a gastroenterologist and a pathologist who are experienced in diagnosing celiac disease can reduce many of the reasons for false negative and false positive biopsy results.

Readers may wonder if blood tests are good enough to replace the need for intestinal biopsies, but celiac disease specialists do not recommend doing this since the TTG IgA blood tests can be abnormal when the intestinal biopsies are normal. Reasons for such false positive TTG IgA tests include autoimmune diseases, liver disease and congestive heart failure. False positive AG IgA and IgG tests are quite common, [and] these tests are no longer recommended in adults when assessing for celiac disease. The DGP antibodies seem less likely to give false positive results, but there is not enough information available yet to know if these in combination with other antibody tests could ever replace the intestinal biopsy for diagnosing celiac disease. I personally do not recommend committing to a gluten-free diet for life especially in children without undergoing definitive (biopsy) testing for celiac disease. . . .

Going Gluten-Free Can Complicate Diagnosis

Going on a gluten-free diet for many months, and particularly for a year or more, can lead to the most commonly used diagnostic tests for celiac disease no longer being helpful. Even intestinal biopsies can go back to a normal or near-normal appearance if you have been gluten-free for a long time. Without an intestinal biopsy that shows the abnormalities of celiac disease, you cannot be diagnosed with celiac disease. . . .

Even if you feel better on a gluten-free diet, this does not mean you have celiac disease. One study showed that only 36 percent of patients who felt better on a gluten-free diet actually had celiac disease. Often, feeling better without gluten in your diet is transient, and then you are left not knowing the true cause of your problem.

Another reason for not going on a gluten-free diet without a true diagnosis of celiac disease is that it may encourage family members to be screened for the disease, even though you may not really have it. As Lara Field, pediatric dietitian specializing in celiac disease

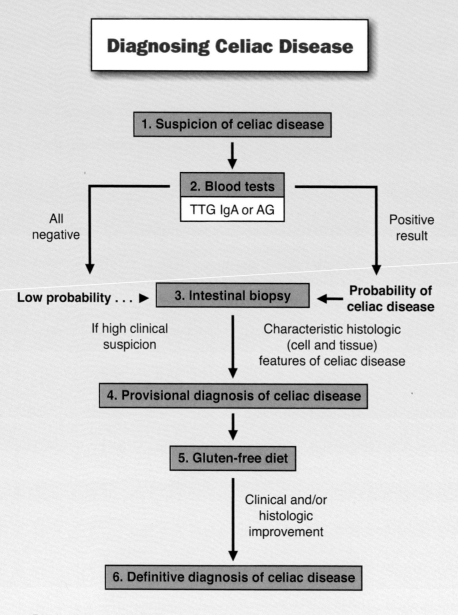

Diagnosing Celiac Disease

1. Suspicion of celiac disease

2. Blood tests
TTG IgA or AG

All negative

Positive result

Low probability ... ▶ **3. Intestinal biopsy** ◀ **Probability of celiac disease**

If high clinical suspicion

Characteristic histologic (cell and tissue) features of celiac disease

4. Provisional diagnosis of celiac disease

5. Gluten-free diet

Clinical and/or histologic improvement

6. Definitive diagnosis of celiac disease

Taken from: Armin Alaedini and Peter H.R. Green, "Narrative Review: Celiac Disease; Understanding a Complex Autoimmune Disorder," *Annals of Internal Medicine*, vol.142, no. 4, February 15, 2005.

at the University of Chicago points out, going gluten-free can also lead to certain nutritional deficiencies, so you should be certain of the diagnosis before committing you[rself]—and perhaps your entire family—to this diet. Studies in the United States, Canada and the U.K.

also show that the cost of eating gluten-free products is two to three times greater than comparable gluten-containing products. So taking on this extra expense without being certain such treatment is necessary may not be a wise financial decision. Of course, if a diagnosis of celiac disease is confirmed, treatment with a gluten-free diet is mandatory. In that case, I encourage working with a knowledgeable dietitian/nutritionist to help you in your quest to eat a balanced and nutritious gluten-free diet.

The only way to make a diagnosis of celiac disease after starting a gluten-free diet is to go back on gluten. This is referred to as a "gluten challenge." . . . However, this may not be necessary if gluten has been avoided for a short time or if gluten was only partially eliminated from the diet. I always check a TTG IgA level when someone comes to see me for possible celiac disease, even if they are eating gluten-free. If this test is positive, then we proceed to endoscopy with intestinal biopsies. Another useful test to check when someone is on a gluten-free diet is the genetic test for celiac disease. . . . If a patient does not have the genes that predispose them to celiac disease, then they cannot have celiac disease and a gluten challenge is not needed. If the genetic test is positive, then going back on gluten is an option in order to make a diagnosis of celiac disease.

The Importance of Genetic Testing for Celiac Disease

The University of Chicago Celiac Disease Center

In the following viewpoint, the University of Chicago Celiac Disease Center asserts that when an individual is diagnosed with celiac disease, his or her entire family should be tested for the presence of DQ2 and DQ8, the two genes most strongly associated with the disorder. According to the author, celiac disease is genetic, so the family members of diagnosed individuals have an increased risk for having the disease. If family members test positive for either of the two genes, they should be monitored, but it does not mean they will develop celiac disease, only that they have a greater risk than the average person. If family members test negative for both genes, they should not ever have to worry about having celiac disease.

The University of Chicago Celiac Disease Center is dedicated to raising awareness and diagnosis rates nationwide and meeting the critical needs of people affected by celiac disease through education, research, and advocacy.

When an individual is diagnosed with celiac disease, the entire family learns that they must be tested on a regular basis for the condition, for they are now at risk. First degree relatives (parent, child, sibling) have a 1 in 22 chance of developing celiac disease in their lifetimes; in second degree relatives, (aunt, uncle, cousin, grandparent) the risk is 1 in 39. Only lifetime screening can help family members reduce the long term impact of celiac disease and facilitate a quick diagnosis. They learn that regular antibody testing is necessary because celiac disease is a genetic condition and could appear again in the family at any time.

The Benefits of Genetic Testing

There is a blood test available to determine whether or not an at-risk individual carries the genes responsible for the development of celiac disease. These genes are located on the HLA-class II complex and are called DQ2 and DQ8. Each case of celiac disease has been found to show these so-called "haplotypes"; therefore, a negative gene test indicates that celiac disease cannot develop in that individual.

There are two main reasons for using the genetic test when evaluating an individual for celiac disease. The first case is to "rule out" celiac disease, which is a medical term that indicates an individual does not possess a necessary risk factor for the development of celiac disease, genetic predisposition. Without this factor, it is impossible that the individual with a negative gene test will develop celiac disease in the future. People who test negative for the gene would *not* be required to have regular antibody screening for the remainder of their lives. For example, the children of an adult with celiac disease could have the gene test. The results would allow the parent to know which children need close monitoring.

> **FAST FACT**
>
> About 30 percent of the population carries genes that make them vulnerable to celiac disease.

The Celiac Disease Center at the University of Chicago recommends that when an individual is diagnosed with celiac disease, the entire family should be tested for the presence of DQ2 and DQ8, two genes associated with the disease. (© Health Protection Agency/Photo Researchers, Inc.)

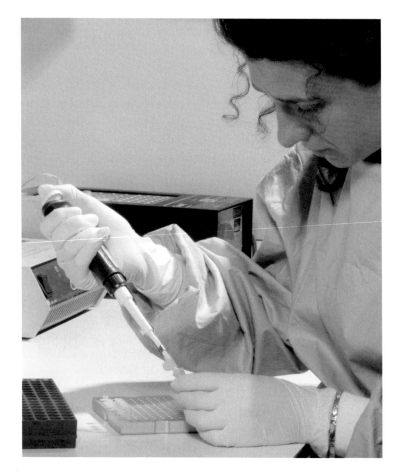

In individuals with symptoms who have not had a biopsy to diagnose celiac disease, but have been on the gluten-free diet for a significant period of time, the gene test is often the only way to determine if symptoms could possibly be related to celiac disease. For a person who faces this situation, a negative gene test would indicate that symptoms are not the a result of celiac disease. A positive gene test, however, does not diagnose the disease but increases the likelihood that it is present. . . .

Testing for Celiac Disease

The gene test does not diagnose celiac disease. It places an individual into an "at-risk" group for celiac disease, which indicates the individual should be closely monitored with antibody testing in the future. When the genetic predisposition for celiac disease was detected (on Chromosome 6) researchers noted that the genes were a necessary but not sufficient condition for the disease to develop. In fact, up to one third of the U.S. population has the genes for celiac disease, but it is thought that only 1–4% of them will actually develop the disease at some point in their lifetimes. This means that people with DQ2 or DQ8 can develop celiac disease, but the vast majority of them aren't *destined* to develop it. . . .

The blood tests that most people with celiac disease are familiar with are the antibody tests. These tests, such as the tissue transglutaminase test (tTG) or the antiendomysial (EMA) antibody test, measure the autoimmune response triggered by gluten that occurs at a point in time. (Think of it as a photograph.) These are important tests because they characterize the extent to which the immune system is responding to gluten.

Unlike antibody testing, the HLA gene testing for celiac disease measures the presence or absence of genetically-programmed molecules that are found on the surface of some cells. The HLA gene test for celiac disease can be performed at any time after birth (and even in the cord blood at birth!)—an individual is either born with or without these factors and they do not change over time.

Inheriting a Genetic Predisposition for Celiac Disease

Inheriting the genes for celiac disease occurs differently than the manner in which many genetic traits are passed on. We are accustomed to thinking in terms of dominant or recessive genes which are inherited from both parents and form sets to determine hair color, height, and other human health characteristics. In fact, even though DQ2 and DQ8 are passed on similarly, they are not sufficient to determine the occurrence of the disease, even if they are present in double doses.

The figures below are derived from a study of 437 Italians with celiac disease and 551 Italians without it.

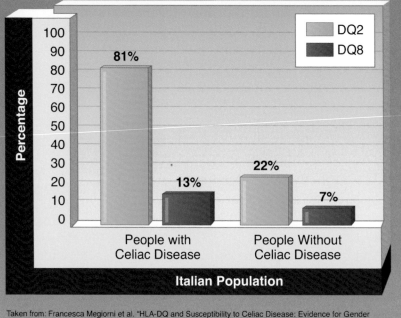

Taken from: Francesca Megiorni et al. "HLA-DQ and Susceptibility to Celiac Disease: Evidence for Gender Differences and Parent-of-Origin Effects, *American Journal of Gastroenterology*, April 2008.

Because 35% of the American population have either DQ2 (more commonly) or DQ8, it is possible for two affected people to marry each other. The genes can be passed on by males as well as females. Therefore, one person's gene test doesn't necessarily mean that the other side of the family is not affected as well.

Genetic testing can be expensive and can vary by geography and the type of medical center where you have it done. Costs include the cost of the actual test, the hospital laboratory fees, equipment/supplies, and processing. The test is usually ordered by a gastroenterologist. . . .

The presence or absence of genetic factors is not influenced by diet.

Celiac Disease Can Affect the Brain

Alicia Woodward

In the following viewpoint, Alicia Woodward asserts that celiac disease can cause neurological and psychological problems. Woodward says most people do not associate celiac disease with brain-related problems, but in people with celiac disease, gluten can cause depression, hallucinations, anxiety, slurred speech, chronic headaches, loss of coordination, or a number of other emotional and neurological problems. According to Woodward, removing gluten from the diet can ease these symptoms if they are caused by celiac disease.

Woodward is a psychotherapist and the editor in chief of *Living Without*, a magazine for people with celiac disease, gluten sensitivity, and food allergies.

K atherine Davis [not her real name], 19, came to my office complaining of low-level depression and heightened anxiety. She worried all the time, she said, and always felt jittery. This anxiety kept her from going out with friends or speaking up in class. A vegetarian whose primary foods, besides salad, were bread, cereal, pasta and yogurt, Katherine confided that she had a "touchy" stomach and suffered frequent bouts of diarrhea, along with chronic gas and bloating. As I asked about her family history, Katherine mentioned that an aunt had similar digestive issues and a cousin had gluten sensitivity. At the end of our session, I gave Katherine an important homework assignment: Get tested for celiac disease.

Celiac disease is a genetic autoimmune disorder characterized by a heightened sensitivity to gluten, the protein in wheat, barley and rye. The disease is more common than most people think, affecting approximately 3 million in the United States, about 1 in 100. One of the most notable things about celiac disease is that up to 97 percent of Americans who have it remain undiagnosed.

Awareness of the disease in the United States is increasing but it can still take years—an average of nine, according to Peter H.R. Green, MD, director of the Celiac Disease Center at Columbia University—to be diagnosed. This may be due to the fact that celiac disease can present with a wide range of subtle to serious symptoms that can vary from person to person. These symptoms include the classic gastrointestinal discomforts commonly associated with the disease—abdominal pain (gas, cramps, bloating), diarrhea or constipation (or both), reflux, unexplained weight loss. In young children, two other well-known symptoms are failure to thrive and abdominal distention. In older children, common symptoms are short stature, anemia and delayed puberty.

But symptoms can also include those not so commonly associated with the disease, such as migraines, seizures, tingling and numbness in the hands or feet, an itchy skin rash, canker sores, clumsiness, "foggy thinking," dementia, fatigue, unexplained weight gain or, as reported by Katherine Davis, anxiety and depression.

Celiac disease symptoms may include migraine headaches and other symptoms not typically associated with the disease. (© **Chris Rout/ Alamy**)

To make diagnosis even more challenging, many patients have no symptoms at all. This phenomenon is known as "the celiac iceberg," in that there are large numbers of celiacs who are completely asymptomatic. These people have either "silent" or "latent" forms of the disease. The key difference is that silent celiacs have obvious intestinal damage (discovered by biopsy of the small intestine via endoscopy) while latent celiacs do not. Both show positive results of the disease in blood-screening tests.

The only treatment for celiac disease is the strict, life-long adherence to a gluten-free diet. If left untreated, the disease damages the lining of the small intestine, affecting and limiting nutrient absorption. Over time, the condition causes malnourishment and all the accompanying symptoms. That's one reason why celiac disease is linked to conditions like iron-deficiency anemia, osteopenia, osteoporosis, vitamin K deficiency and infertility, as well as other autoimmune disorders like type 1 diabetes and rheumatoid arthritis.

Gluten and the Brain

It makes sense to me to view celiac disease—and the broader, as yet ill-defined condition known as "gluten sensitivity"—as having three different presentations that may or may not occur together. That's (1) celiac disease in the traditional sense with gut damage to the small bowel; (2) skin problems—an itchy rash called dermatitis herpetiformis, or DH; and (3) brain-related issues—neurologic and psychological problems. All three are treated with the gluten-free diet.

Of these three, the brain-related aspects of the disease are the least well known by the general public and the medical community. Doctors often look for the obvious gastrointestinal distress and dismiss neurologic and emotional symptoms, which can lead to delayed diagnosis and unnecessary suffering.

"Patients and their doctors should know that certain chronic neurological disorders are due to celiac disease," said Stefano Guandalini, MD, the medical director of the University of Chicago Celiac Disease Center, in an interview with *Living Without* magazine. "Some syndromes, like epilepsy with calcification in the brain, are definitely linked to celiac disease. If you look at other neurological disorders—epilepsy without a known cause, ataxia (unstable gait, clumsiness), peripheral neuropathy (tingling or numbness

FAST FACT

Gluten sensitivity can be primarily and at times exclusively a neurological disease, according to neurologist Marios Hadjivassiliou from the University of Sheffield in England.

in the hands or feet), or even recurrent headaches—you'll find a higher than expected percentage of these patients have celiac disease."

When the focus of celiac activity is in the brain, a patient can develop problems with walking, speaking and swallowing. This is because the gluten reaction, called gluten ataxia, targets the cerebellum, the center that controls coordination and complex movements. Often, the peripheral nerves located outside the spinal cord are also involved, leading to chronic and progressive neuropathy, a disease affecting the nervous system that results in feelings of numbness, tingling or pain. Other neurologic symptoms are slurred speech, loss of coordination in upper and lower limbs, difficultly with normal walking, vision problems, chronic headaches. In children and young adults, you may see developmental delay, diminished muscle tone, learning disorders and ADHD [attention-deficit/hyperactivity disorder] symptoms.

Celiac disease can even present as autistic-like behavior. "Autism and celiac disease are distinct, unrelated entities but some autistic-like behaviors, especially in young children, are associated with celiac disease. An undiagnosed child may, in fact, appear sad, introverted, unwilling to socialize or communicate even with his or her parents or the child may be cranky and excessively irritable." said Guandalini.

In addition, brain-related symptoms of celiac disease can be psychiatric in nature. "It's well documented in medical literature. Hallucinations, depression, anxiety, suicide ideation—they're all associated with celiac disease," Guandalini said. "Fortunately, these symptoms, including depression, anxiety and hallucinations, promptly regress on a gluten-free diet."

Getting Screened

The incidence of celiac disease is higher in groups of people who have certain medical conditions. For example,

Neurological Disorders and Celiac Disease

Studies show that the occurrence of neurological issues is usually greater in patients with celiac disease (CD) than in control subjects.

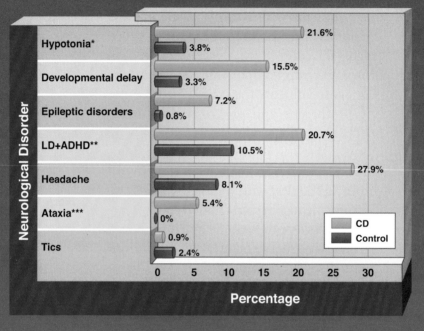

*Hypotonia: low muscle tone
**LD+ADHD: learning disability+attention-deficit/hyperactivity disorder
***Ataxia: lack of coordination

Taken from: Nathanel Zelnik et al. "Range of Neurologic Disorders in Patients with Celiac Disease," *Pediatrics*, June 1, 2004.

8 to 10 percent of patients with type 1 diabetes have celiac disease.

Over 10 percent of individuals with Down syndrome also have celiac disease. The disease often remains undiagnosed in this vulnerable population as those with Down can have trouble verbalizing what can be vague symptoms. Caregivers are encouraged to look for subtle signs of discomfort or periods of "being off" in terms of behavior, attitude or reduced energy levels. Periodic testing is recommended for those with Down syndrome.

Others at higher risk for celiac disease include people with the following conditions:

- First-degree relatives with biopsy-proven celiac disease
- Addison's disease
- Graves' disease
- Hashimoto's thyroiditis
- Selective IgA Deficiency
- Sjögren's disease
- Turner's syndrome
- Unexplained infertility or recurrent miscarriage
- Williams syndrome

The most common screening test for celiac disease is the anti-tissue transglutaminase (tTG-IgA). Anyone with IgA deficiency (a blood condition that can skew screening results) should undergo a total serum IgA test. Other blood tests for celiac include the antiendomysial antibody (EMA-IgA) and the new deamidated gliadin peptide (DGP).

Even with a negative test result, experts suggest that these populations be re-tested at regular intervals. A positive result indicates that a person needs a biopsy; it is not a diagnosis. The diagnostic gold standard is endoscopic biopsy of the small intestine, which confirms damaged villi.

Celiac medical experts strongly recommend that people be screened for celiac disease before embarking on the gluten-free diet. The reason for this is that test results are not accurate unless the patient has been eating a regular (gluten-containing) diet for a period before being tested.

There's a genetic test available that looks for two celiac markers: HLA-DQ2 and HLA-DQ8. A positive finding does not indicate a celiac diagnosis but a negative result can help rule out the disease. Note that eating gluten (or not) before this test does not affect test results.

And what about Katherine Davis, my anxious patient with the "touchy" stomach? Katherine and I addressed her anxiety and depression with cognitive-behavior therapy. But this treatment didn't ease her symptoms like the change she ultimately made to her diet. After a blood screening showed heightened antibodies to gluten, Katherine underwent an intestinal biopsy and received a celiac diagnosis. Within days of going gluten-free, her stomach problems disappeared, her depression lifted and her anxiety faded to manageable levels. She is going out with friends, volunteering regularly in class—and is no longer my patient.

Potential New Treatments for Celiac Disease

Cathryn Delude

In the following viewpoint, Cathryn Delude describes scientists' efforts to find a nondietary treatment for celiac disease. Currently, the only way to treat celiac disease is by modifying one's diet to eliminate gluten. According to Delude, one approach scientists are taking is the creation of a vaccine that will help train the body to tolerate gluten. Other approaches include the use of bacterial enzymes to break gluten down before it reaches the intestine and the use of hookworms to try to dull the immune response to gluten.

Delude writes about science and medicine for magazines and newspapers and also for hospitals and universities. Her articles have appeared in the *Los Angeles Times, Boston Globe, New York Times, Scientific American,* and other publications.

I n a sense, the 2 million plus Americans with celiac disease are lucky. No other autoimmune disease has such a safe and effective treatment.

SOURCE: Cathryn Delude, "New Hope for Celiac Disease Sufferers?," *Los Angeles Times,* December 21, 2009. www.articles.latimes.com. Copyright © 2009 by Los Angeles Times. All rights reserved. Reproduced by permission.

Purging the diet of gluten—the protein in wheat, rye and barley that triggers an immune reaction in the gut—can reverse the disease and reduce intestinal inflammation. That's important, because studies now show that the consequences of untreated celiac disease are graver than previously thought, causing anemia, arthritis, osteoporosis, hepatitis, neurological problems and even malignancies, as well as increased general mortality.

Still, it is very difficult to eliminate gluten entirely. It lurks in disparate sources such as vinegars, soy sauce, medications, lip balm and Play-Doh (which some children consider edible); and even gluten-free foods, which are expensive, may contain enough traces to cause symptoms. "When we study celiac patients who have been doing their best to follow a gluten-free diet, even after five years we see lots of damage in the small intestines in about half of them," said Dr. Robert Anderson, a gastroenterologist in Melbourne, Australia, who is working on a vaccine to prevent or switch off the reaction to gluten.

His is one of many efforts under way to develop new, non-dietary treatments for celiac disease. Ultimately, celiac patients may be able to take a pill before a meal so they could, for example, have stuffing with their holiday turkey. Or, as is Anderson's goal, they could go for a series of treatments similar to allergy shots that would teach their immune systems to tolerate gluten.

"It's very exciting that the pathophysiology of celiac disease is understood to such a degree that we can design potential therapies," said Dr. Peter Green, director of the Celiac Disease Center at Columbia University College of Physicians and Surgeons in New York.

There are two categories of treatments being developed. One would supplement a gluten-free diet and protect patients from occasional gluten exposure; the other would train the immune system to tolerate gluten and allow patients to eat a regular diet.

Enzyme Therapy

Within the first category, one approach uses oral enzymes that target gluten. We cannot completely digest gluten because humans lack digestive enzymes that can break it down, but researchers at Stanford University combined enzymes from bacteria and barley that finish

Clinical Trial Results: An Oral Enzyme Therapy Appears Promising

CD patients' intestines were biopsied, and the organ's nutrient-absorbing villi were measured. Then about half of the patients were given an oral enzyme therapy (ALN003), and the rest received a placebo (sugar pill). All patients were given certain amounts of gluten. After six weeks, their intestines were biopsied again and the villi were remeasured. The patients receiving ALV003 sustained less damage to their villi. Although this illustration is not drawn to scale, it does demonstrate the gross structural difference between healthy villi (taller) and gluten-damaged villi.

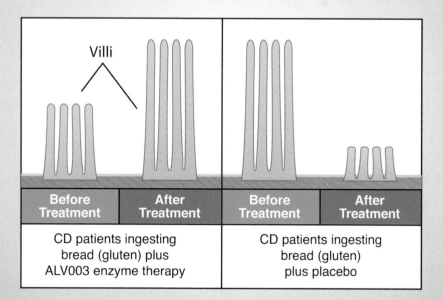

Before Treatment	After Treatment	Before Treatment	After Treatment
CD patients ingesting bread (gluten) plus ALV003 enzyme therapy		CD patients ingesting bread (gluten) plus placebo	

Taken from: Markku Mäki, "ALV003, a Novel Glutenase, Attenuates Gluten-Induced Small Intestinal Mucosal Injury in Celiac Disease Patents: A Randomized Controlled Phase 2A Clinical Trial," Abstract no. 0P050b, Nineteenth United European Gastroenterology Week, Stockholm, Sweden, October 24, 2011.

what our own digestive juices cannot. They showed in rats that when gluten is broken down into smaller fragments, it no longer causes inflammation in the intestines. Alvine Pharmaceuticals, based in San Carlos, Calif., has developed this "glutenase" therapy and is now recruiting patients for a Phase II clinical trial.

In this trial, as with the others, participants have had a diagnosis of celiac disease confirmed by a biopsy but have had it under control on a gluten-free diet. They are given either a drug or placebo, along with a gluten challenge, often the equivalent of one or two slices of bread.

FAST FACT

Most adults are diagnosed with celiac disease between the ages of thirty and fifty years old.

"From the early data it looks like the oral enzymes break down enough gluten to be useful," said Dr. Daniel Leffler, director of clinical research for the Celiac Center at Beth Israel Deaconess Medical Center in Boston. Leffler was not involved in the enzyme trial but is an investigator in a nearly completed Phase II trial testing a different drug, larazotide, developed by Alba Therapeutics in Maryland.

The larazotide approach leaves the gluten peptides, or small fragments of proteins, intact but aims to prevent them from penetrating beneath the lining of the gut into the mucous layer where the immune reaction occurs. In celiac disease, as in many autoimmune diseases, including Type 1 diabetes, this intestinal barrier is "leaky" or permeable.

Larazotide is a bioengineered drug designed to close those leaks to keep out gluten and prevent or reverse the disease. In preliminary results from about 300 patients in Phase I and II trials, the drug did seem to benefit patients, who had fewer adverse symptoms after eating gluten. It also reduced the levels of the antibody that serves as a blood marker for the immune response to gluten. But interestingly, the drug did not seem to reduce intestinal permeability.

"So the drug works, but maybe through a different mechanism that we don't understand yet," said Green, who is on the clinical advisory board for both Alba and Alvine. He predicts that, if ultimately found effective, the oral enzymes and larazotide would be marketed as supplements to a gluten-free diet but that many patients would want them to actually replace the restrictive diet. It's unclear not only whether such a use would be possible but also whether it would be a daily regimen or followed only when dining out or traveling, for instance.

Immunotherapy

The second category of treatment, known as immunotherapy, is more investigational but also more exciting, Leffler said. It would allow patients to eat a regular diet by quelling immune response in the gut. This response is driven by immune cells known as T cells, which react when other immune cells display gluten fragments on their surface.

In Australia, a company founded by Anderson, called Nexpep, is packaging the gluten peptides that trigger this immune response into a vaccine that will desensitize the immune reaction. The theory, which he says works in animals, is that by introducing these peptides through injections under the skin rather than through the gut, the immune cells learn to tolerate them and no longer display them to the T cells. That can theoretically prevent or turn off the reaction that damages the intestines. Anderson expects Phase I safety trials of this vaccine, Nexvax2, to be completed in mid-2010. He anticipates that patients would receive a series of injections of the vaccine, followed by occasional maintenance doses.

"If we can figure out how to give the drug, how frequently and when we need maintenance therapy," he added, "then we can use the same principle to explore treatments for other autoimmune diseases." Several other groups are also developing vaccines for celiac disease, but this one is furthest along.

The hookworm (pictured), an intestinal parasite, has been found to be helpful in treating celiac symptoms. (© David Scharf/Photo Researchers, Inc.)

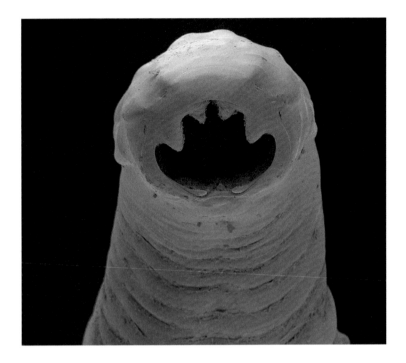

A low-tech immunotherapy approach might require just one inoculation—of hookworm. It is known that a non-pathogenic hookworm introduced to the gut can relieve asthma symptoms. Researchers suspect that it is because we evolved with intestinal parasites that trained our immune system to tolerate environmental irritants, but our hygienic modern living has deprived us of this beneficial symbiosis.

Researchers at the Brisbane Princess Alexandra Hospital in Queensland, Australia, tested the effects of hookworm inoculation on 20 patients with celiac disease to see if it would blunt the immune response to gluten. In addition to hoping to provide relief for celiac patients, the researchers want to learn if this could be an effective therapy for inflammatory bowel disease and Crohn's disease. The results have not been published, but when the Phase II trial was over and the patients were offered a medication that would kill the parasites, they all opted to keep their hookworms.

Gluten Sensitivity Is Distinct from Celiac Disease

Alessio Fasano, as told to Alicia Woodward

In the following viewpoint, Alicia Woodward of *Living Without* magazine interviews Alessio Fasano, the lead investigator of a groundbreaking study that found that gluten sensitivity and celiac disease are distinct immune-related diseases. This finding is very important, says Fasano, particularly for those individuals who suffer from gluten intolerance but who test negative for celiac disease. Many of these people were labeled as hypochondriacs, he asserts. He says his study shows that these people are likely to suffer from gluten sensitivity. According to Fasano, gluten sensitivity—and wheat allergy, another related disease—have many of the same symptoms of celiac disease; however, the immunological causes of the diseases are completely different.

Fasano is a professor of pediatric medicine at the University of Maryland School of Medicine and the director of the Center for Celiac Research.

*[A*licia Woodward for] Living Without: *Thanks to your team's research, we now know that gluten sensitivity actually exists. What does this mean to the gluten-free community?*

Alessio Fasano: In my humble opinion, it's a big deal. First, we've moved gluten sensitivity, also called gluten intolerance, from a nebulous condition to a distinct entity—and one that's very distinct from celiac disease. Gluten sensitivity affects 6 to 7 times more people than celiac disease so the impact is tremendous. Second, we now understand that reactions to gluten are on a spectrum. The immune system responds to gluten in different ways depending on who you are and your genetic disposition. Third, there's a lot of confusion in terms of gluten reactions. Gluten and autism, gluten and schizophrenia—is there a link or not? These debates are on their way to being settled. And fourth and most important, for the first time we can advise those people who test negative for celiac disease but insist they're having a bad reaction to gluten that there may be something there, that they're not making it up, that they're not hypochondriacs. Once it's established that a patient has a bad reaction to gluten, it's important to determine which part of the spectrum he or she is on before engaging in treatment, which is the gluten-free diet.

FAST FACT

Children can outgrow a wheat allergy, but not celiac disease.

Different Diseases

Do you believe people can move along this spectrum? Could someone be gluten sensitive and then develop celiac disease?

No, I don't think so. The three main conditions—celiac disease, gluten sensitivity, wheat allergy—are based on very different mechanisms in the immune system. Given that fact, it's hard to imagine the possibility that you could jump from one to the other.

Yet many of the symptoms of gluten sensitivity and celiac disease are the same.

That's right. While there's a clear distinction on the immunological side, there's tremendous overlap on the clinical side. If you came to my clinic complaining of tingling in your fingers or depression or headaches from eating gluten, these symptoms (and many others) are associated with celiac disease. If your celiac tests are negative, these same symptoms could point to gluten sensitivity. There's no question about that.

Up to 20 million Americans may have gluten sensitivity. That's in addition to 3 million who have celiac disease and 400,000 to 600,000 with wheat allergy. Humans have consumed wheat as a staple tor generations. What's going on?

Although we've been eating wheat for thousands of years, we are not engineered to digest gluten. We are able

This rash was caused by a gluten intolerance. Gluten intolerance is distinct from celiac disease, although the symptoms are similar. (© PHANIE/Photo Researchers, Inc.)

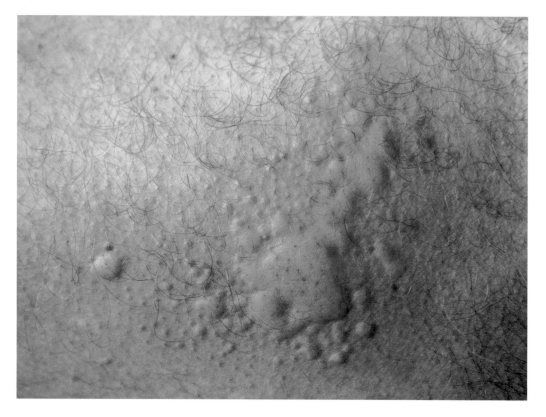

to completely digest every protein we put in our mouths with the exception of one—and that's gluten. Gluten is a weird protein. We don't have the enzymes to dismantle it completely, leaving undigested peptides that can be harmful. The immune system may perceive them as an enemy and mount an immune response.

An Increase in Gluten-Related Problems

It seems like we're seeing an explosion of gluten-related health problems.

Two components are coming together to create this perfect storm. First, the grains we're eating have changed dramatically. In our great-grandparents era, wheat con-

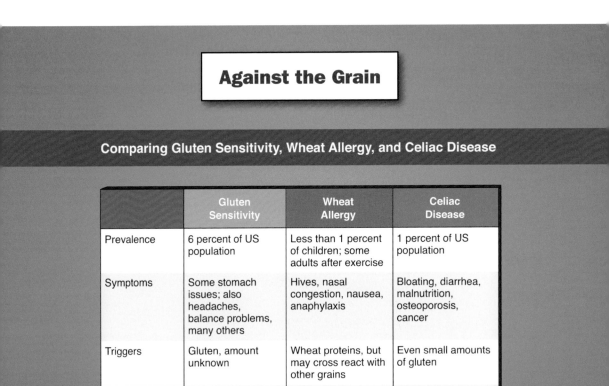

Against the Grain

Comparing Gluten Sensitivity, Wheat Allergy, and Celiac Disease

	Gluten Sensitivity	Wheat Allergy	Celiac Disease
Prevalence	6 percent of US population	Less than 1 percent of children; some adults after exercise	1 percent of US population
Symptoms	Some stomach issues; also headaches, balance problems, many others	Hives, nasal congestion, nausea, anaphylaxis	Bloating, diarrhea, malnutrition, osteoporosis, cancer
Triggers	Gluten, amount unknown	Wheat proteins, but may cross react with other grains	Even small amounts of gluten
Treatment	Gluten-free diet, although small amounts may be tolerable	Avoid wheat products	Strict gluten-free diet

Taken from: Melinda Beck, "Clues to Gluten Sensitivity," *Wall Street Journal*, March 15, 2011.
http://online.wsj.com/article/SB10001424052748704893604576200393522456636.html.

tained very low amounts of gluten and it was harvested once a year. Now we've engineered our grains to substantially increase yields and contain characteristics, like more elasticity, that we like. We're susceptible to the consequences of these extremely rich, gluten-containing grains. Second, and this applies to the prevalence of celiac disease that's increased 4-fold in the last 40 years, is the upward trend we're seeing in all autoimmune diseases. We're changing our environment faster than our bodies can adapt to it.

You mentioned the link between gluten and conditions like autism and schizophrenia. Can you elaborate?

This is very controversial. Some people believe undisputedly that gluten plays a role in these kinds of conditions while others say that's bogus. Most likely the truth is in the middle. I have a hard time believing that all kids with autism improve once they go on a gluten-free diet. At the same time, I have a hard time believing that gluten has absolutely nothing to do with these behaviors. We know in clinic that people can have behavioral issues due to gluten, such as short-term memory loss, mood swings, depression, so you can imagine schizophrenic and autistic behaviors. If it's true, as I believe, that complex diseases like autism are final destinations but that you can take different paths to get there, I have to believe that one of those paths for a subgroup of patients could, in fact, be gluten sensitivity.

Is there a test for gluten sensitivity?

No. So far, the only way to determine gluten sensitivity is an exclusion diagnosis. You have a problem with gluten. The problem goes away when you go on a gluten-free diet and comes back when you add gluten back into your diet.

What would you advise someone who believes they're gluten sensitive, given there isn't a conclusive test right now?

Do not try the gluten-free diet before you see your physician. You must exclude a celiac diagnosis before you start the diet. If celiac disease and wheat allergy and all other causes of your symptoms have been excluded, then and only then is it worthwhile to do a gluten-free trial.

Should One Avoid Gluten?

Do you recommend that most people avoid gluten, provided they get tested for celiac disease first?

I wouldn't go to this extreme because the gluten-free diet isn't a walk in the park. The bottom line is quality of life. If you're suffering with symptoms that make your life miserable and you've investigated all possible causes, including celiac disease, I don't see anything wrong with going on the gluten-free diet. If you're gluten sensitive, you'll see quick improvement on the diet, a matter of days or weeks at the most. It's not weeks, months or years like with celiac disease.

Having said that, at the clinic we take care of athletes who are healthy but say they feel much more energetic and have increased endurance on the gluten-free diet. Novak Djokovic, the tennis star who's gluten sensitive, claims his endurance, capability to concentrate and energy have skyrocketed since going gluten-free.

I've heard you say that gluten sensitivity is where celiac disease was 30 years ago.

It's déjà vu. The patients, as usual, were visionary, telling us this stuff existed but healthcare professionals were skeptical. The confusion surrounding gluten sensitivity—testing, biomarkers—is exactly the same confusion we had around celiac disease 30 years ago. So we're starting all over again now.

Moving Toward Prevention

What's surprised you most about the studies you've conducted?

I was shocked to learn that certain people have tricks that allow them to tolerate gluten for 60 or 70 years without getting sick—and then suddenly in their mid-70s, they develop celiac disease. This means it's not destiny. You're not born to develop celiac disease. That's mind-blowing to me. So I'm dying to know what kind of tricks these people use to tolerate gluten for so long. If we learn the tricks, we can apply them to everybody at risk for the disease and put them in a stage of tolerance so they'd never get the disease. And here's another thing—why do they suddenly lose this trick? If we knew, we could use that knowledge to avoid other problems. Celiac disease is a prototype of other conditions, like diabetes, multiple sclerosis, rheumatoid arthritis, cancer, heart attack, stroke. The mechanism is all the same. So if we can understand what the heck is going on with celiac disease, it could lead to huge, huge changes in preventive medicine.

CHAPTER 2

Controversies Concerning Celiac Disease

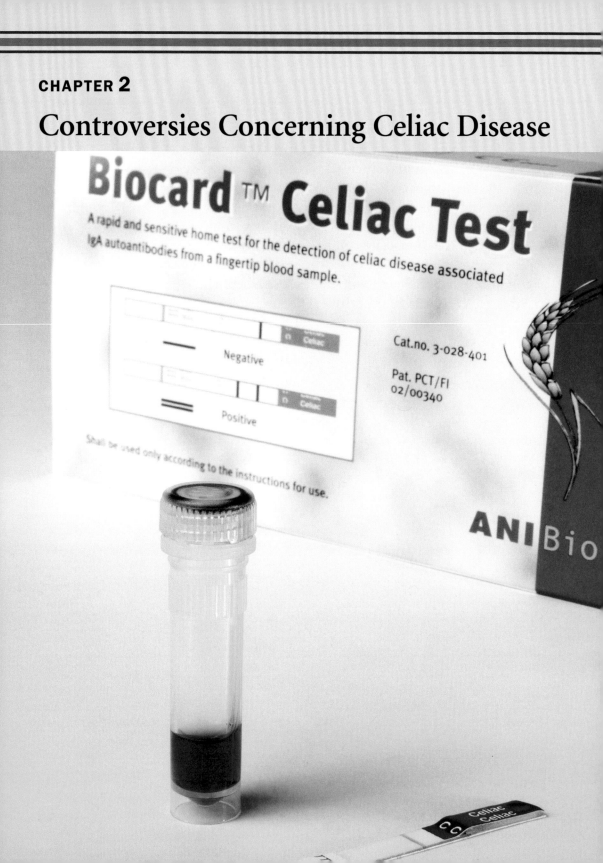

Celiac Disease: A Hidden Epidemic

Peter H.R. Green

In the following viewpoint, taken from his book *Celiac Disease: A Hidden Epidemic*, Peter H.R. Green argues that celiac disease is one of the most common and underdiagnosed hereditary autoimmune conditions in the United States. According to Green, millions of Americans suffer from the wide-ranging symptoms associated with celiac disease. However, most of them find no relief from their symptoms because they are misdiagnosed or even dismissed by doctors. Usually, says Green, people suffer for years before celiac disease is diagnosed. He likens celiac disease to an iceberg silently moving across the United States, burdening people with various ailments and placing them at risk for long-term complications.

Green is a professor of clinical medicine at the College of Physicians and Surgeons, Columbia University, an attending physician at New York–Presbyterian Hospital, and the director of the Columbia University Celiac Disease Center.

Photo on facing page. Millions of people in the United States have undiagnosed celiac disease. For people who suspect they have the disease, a number of tests are available for use at home. (© Cordelia Molloy/Photo Researchers, Inc.)

SOURCE: Peter H.R. Green, M.D., and Rory Jones, "Introduction," *Celiac Disease: A Hidden Epidemic*, 2006, pp. 1–4. New York: HarperCollins. Copyright © 2010 by HarperCollins Publishers. All rights reserved. Reproduced by permission of the publisher and the authors.

What's Wrong with Me?

My doctor kept treating my symptoms, but never figured out why my stomach was always upset. I started getting migraines and then joint pain and . . . well, you name it. I was a walking pharmacy and still felt lousy. (Marg, 47)*

My daughter was always tired. It was a joke with her friends—where's Mel—she's asleep. She slept through classes in college . . . it affected her social life. We even did an overnight sleep study in the hospital—she was sleeping fourteen to sixteen hours a day. (Roni)

My daughter had legs like pick-up sticks and an enormous belly and the pediatrician called it "baby fat" and said she'd grow into it. (Mike, 40)

I think people thought I was a hypochondriac—there was so much wrong with me. (Heather, 43)

In the United States today, millions of patients suffer with symptoms that neither fit a specific diagnosis nor disappear. Young and old take drugs and see numerous specialists for gastrointestinal complaints, anemia, joint pain, itchy skin conditions, constant fatigue, or headaches. Their symptoms are treated, but no underlying cause can be found. One doctor diagnoses fibromyalgia, another chronic fatigue syndrome, a third irritable bowel syndrome. Too much or too little roughage, lactose or fructose intolerance, fried or spicy food explains repeated bouts of reflux, diarrhea, constipation, abdominal pain, and gas. Muscle strain or the "wrong type of mattress" is the excuse for aching joints or tingling extremities that remain asleep when the rest of you wakes up in the morning.

Frustrated, patients seek care from "alternative" nontraditional physicians because a friend or neighbor got

---

* In order to preserve patient confidentiality we have used first names or pseudonyms throughout. Some patients declined to have their ages listed.

help there or the physician appeared on TV. Hundreds of dollars later—after a battery of blood or stool tests that most traditional physicians will not even review once they see the name of the laboratory that performed them—the diagnosis comes down to "leaky" gut or too much of the wrong bacteria. Trials of antibacterial agents, expensive intravenous vitamin infusions, multiple herbal remedies, or low-yeast diets all seem the answer. They provide a temporary respite when well-trained physicians cannot provide an answer.

> ## FAST FACT
>
> About 4.5 times as many people have celiac disease today than did during the 1950s, according to a 2009 study.

Six or seven years into this downward physical and mental spiral, an internist suggests that stress may be the answer. In other words, we cannot find anything really wrong with you— perhaps it is "in your head." Many patients live in a perpetual state of indefinable ill health that, after a period of time, they begin to accept as normal. Some of the symptoms seem to "run in the family."

> *I've had it* [reflux and dyspepsia] *for so long that I just think it's a normal part of my life. My mother has it, my brother has it. So, I just assume it's what I'm supposed to have.* (Cindy, 45)

For many patients, there is a medical diagnosis for the bundle of symptoms they must endure. Diagnosis and treatment of this condition will not only improve your health, it may save your life.

The Celiac Iceberg

Celiac disease is a multisystem disorder whose primary target of injury is the small intestine. The disease is triggered by gluten, the main storage protein found in certain grains. Gluten damages the small intestine so that it is unable to absorb nutrients properly. As food malabsorption continues and the disease progresses, the manifestations inevitably become more varied and complex.

The visible peak of the iceberg above water represents people with symptoms of celiac disease. The first submerged part of the iceberg represents people who have the intestinal damage of celiac diseases but no symptoms. The lowest part of the iceberg represents people who are genetically predisposed to celiac disease but who have no symptoms or intestinal damage.

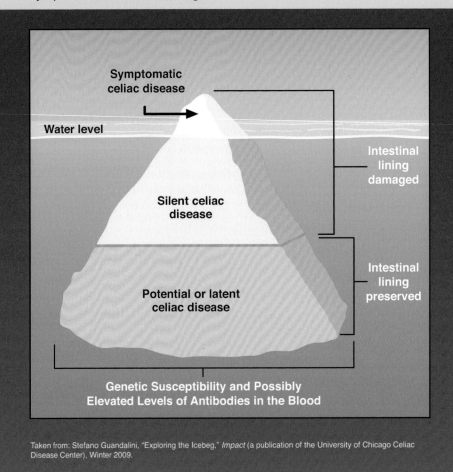

Taken from: Stefano Guandalini, "Exploring the Icebeg," *Impact* (a publication of the University of Chicago Celiac Disease Center), Winter 2009.

Celiac disease is the most common—and one of the most underdiagnosed—hereditary autoimmune conditions in the United States today. It is as common as hereditary high cholesterol.

Once considered a rare "diarrheal" disease of childhood, celiac disease is now recognized predominantly as a disease of adults—and the majority of people are either asymptomatic or consult doctors for a variety of other complaints.

While the disease is considered common in Europe, South America, Canada, and Australia—a recent study of schoolchildren in Finland showed the incidence to be 1 per 99, in parts of England 1 per 100—*only recently have studies shown that celiac disease affects approximately 1 percent of the U.S. population (approximately 1 in every 100 people)—and 97 percent of them are undiagnosed.* Unfortunately, if the disease progresses and is not diagnosed until later in adulthood, patients often develop many other problems from years of inflammation and the malabsorption of minerals, vitamins, and other necessary nutrients.

A delay in diagnosis also increases the chances of developing associated autoimmune diseases. Most adults with celiac disease have bone loss, resulting in osteopenia or osteoporosis. Anemia, malignancies, peripheral neuropathies (numb and/or tingling extremities), dental enamel defects, hyposplenism (underactive spleen), and infertility are also secondary conditions associated with the disease.

Since patients with one autoimmune disease are more likely to have or to develop another, patients with celiac disease are also seen with Sjögren's syndrome, type 1 diabetes, autoimmune thyroid disease, dermatitis herpetiformis (an intensely itchy skin condition) or alopecia areata (a condition that causes hair loss). *Of the 2.1 million people with type 1 diabetes, 8 to 10 percent also have celiac disease.*

Often, people are treated for an autoimmune condition before being diagnosed with celiac disease.

Unfortunately, there is an increased mortality rate for people with celiac disease, exceeding that of the general population, due mainly to malignancies. Current research shows a statistical risk that is 33 times greater for small intestinal adenocarcinoma, 11.6 times greater for esophageal cancer, 9.1 times greater for non-Hodgkin's lymphoma, 5 times greater for melanoma, and 23 times greater for papillary thyroid cancer.

In the United States today, *the average time to diagnosis of celiac disease is currently nine years*—a time frame that the authors personally know to be both accurate and about eight years too long. Patients normally see numerous physicians and specialists for symptoms that are misdiagnosed, do not respond to drug therapy, or are treated without concern for their underlying cause. Young children may suffer for one-third to one-half their lifetime before obtaining a diagnosis.

A majority of people in the United States have a "silent" variety of celiac disease. Without marked gastrointestinal symptoms, many of these patients are diagnosed with celiac disease concurrent with another diagnosis, often a malignancy. This scenario also occurs in adults who received a celiac disease diagnosis as a child and whose parents were told they would "grow out of it."

> *I was told by my mom—many, many years ago—that I had celiac disease as a baby. I had severe diarrhea and the doctor put me on a special milk and bananas diet and it went away and that was the end of it. When I was diagnosed with celiac disease two years ago, I said: "I had that as a baby."* (Linda, 62)

You do not outgrow celiac disease. You develop symptoms that point in other medical directions and become part of the iceberg that is "below the waterline" and off the medical radar screens. Patients often see doctors for a myriad of other complaints, and their mild or apparently unrelated symptoms are often only recognized retrospectively.

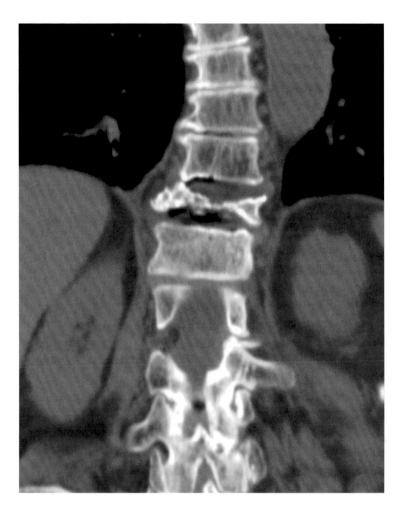

Most adults with celiac disease have a decrease in bone density, or osteoporosis. In this color-enhanced X-ray, osteoporosis has caused a compression fracture in the twelfth thoracic vertebra (shown in blue). (© **Medical Body Scans/ Photo Researchers, Inc.**)

"Why Worry?"

Celiac disease is a significant medical condition. It is far too often masked by or mistaken for a number of more commonly diagnosed conditions. The result is a huge population of patients suffering unnecessarily and at considerable risk for major complications. These patients may also be burdened by depression and complicated professional and family dynamics as a result of their long-term undiagnosed illnesses.

Celiac disease is a huge iceberg that is moving, not quite so silently, across many of our lives.

It Is Likely That the Celiac Disease Epidemic Is Caused by an Infectious Agent

Richard Worzel

Richard Worzel is a futurist, someone who predicts future trends and makes a living helping companies and organizations plan for future events. In the following viewpoint, Worzel contends that there is a celiac disease epidemic and speculates that it is caused by a microbe. He thinks that when people who have a gene predisposing them to celiac disease are exposed to the microbe they suddenly become intolerant to gluten. He also thinks it is likely that other autoimmune diseases are also triggered by microbes.

The world is experiencing another pandemic, this time of a relatively little-known disease. While most people have never heard of celiac disease, they may wind up contracting it, and if enough people get it, it may spell the end of the pizza industry, as well as commercial disaster for the sale of normal breads, cakes, pastries, and other baked goods, plus it will deliver an

SOURCE: Richard Worzel, "The End of Pizza? The Spreading Celiac Epidemic," *Future Search*, February 16, 2010. www.futuresearch.com. Copyright © 2010 by Richard Worzel. All rights reserved. Reproduced by permission.

enormous financial blow to grain farmers. Allow me to first explain, and then speculate.

Celiac disease is one of many different autoimmune diseases. When someone with celiac disease is exposed to a particular protein found in the glutens of wheat, barley, or rye, it triggers the body to attack itself by tearing out the lining of the small intestine. Over time, this will cause someone with celiac disease to suffer from various kinds of malnutrition, because the food eaten is not absorbed by the body. If left untreated for an extended period, this can lead to calcium, iron, vitamin or other deficiencies, and eventually even death from malnutrition. As well, this disease can open up the body to infection and other kinds of problems, such as lymphoma, by lowering the body's natural defenses in the GI tract.

Fortunately, there is a treatment: you don't eat anything made with wheat, barley, rye—or oats, not because oats have the offending protein, but because the machinery that processes oats is almost invariably also used to process the other grains. Celiacs (those who suffer from celiac disease), therefore, follow a very strict regimen of avoiding foods made with these grains—including pizza, and all the other goodies mentioned.

A Global Pandemic of Contagious Celiac Disease

I'm a celiac, and when I was diagnosed more than 20 years ago, I was told that the incidence of celiac disease in North America was less than one person in 2,000 (which was part of the reason why it took my doctors over 3 ½ years to figure out what was wrong with me). Today I'm told that the incidence is 1 in 125, and I've read some research that hints it might be as high as one person in four. Some people say that this is due to greater awareness leading to faster, and more frequent, diagnoses, and that is undoubtedly true. But I also believe there is something else going on, a literal global pandemic of contagious celiac

A woman prepares gluten-free cinnamon rolls. The worldwide increase in celiac disease threatens the baked goods and pizza industries because celiacs cannot tolerate these foods. (© Washington Post/Getty Images)

disease. I have no scientific proof for this; it's a hunch, but let me explain my reasoning.

Not that much is known about celiac disease, in part because it was such a lonely (i.e., infrequently diagnosed) disease, but what is known is that it is genetically-linked. If you don't have a particular gene (as yet unknown), then you (probably) can't get it no matter what. If you do have the gene, then it's thought that some environmental factor triggers this genetic susceptibility, and then for the rest of your life you must avoid wheat, barley, rye, and oats, or suffer the consequences.

The Missing Factor

What no one knows is what the environmental factor is. I believe it's either a particular strain of bacteria, or a virus. I had no apparent signs of celiac disease for decades before I was diagnosed—but you could chalk that up to lack of awareness. One of my nephews had no symptoms at all, until suddenly, when he was 13, he suddenly became quite dramatically intolerant of gluten. Eating something made with gluten made him seriously sick for days—a far more severe reaction than mine. And this intolerance for gluten just appeared out of nowhere, without warning.

Not long ago, my daughter started to show similar signs of gluten intolerance, more like mine than my nephew's. She has yet to be formally diagnosed, but all the symptoms match.

So far, all I've demonstrated is what we already know: that there's a clear genetic link to celiac disease. Yet, in my travels as a futurist, speaker, and consultant (not to mention as a tourist), I've found the awareness of celiac disease has risen dramatically in the last 10 years, and the availability of gluten-free foods has exploded, not just in the U.S. and Canada, but in the United Kingdom, France, Italy, China, the Caribbean, and Australia, where I've worked and traveled. It's almost as if celiac disease is contagious, and is sweeping the world—which is exactly what I think is happening.

FAST FACT

According to the National Foundation for Celiac Awareness, 5 to 22 percent of celiac patients have an immediate family member who also has celiac.

I believe, as I've said, that there is some kind of microbe that induces an infection that is triggering the widespread, but latent, genetic susceptibility for celiac disease. And for some reason, this infection is now sweeping the world. It may be something that a cold bug added to its genetic code somewhere along the line, so that people with the genetic susceptibility who come down with that particular cold also wind up with celiac disease. Then, while they recover from the cold, they never recover from having their genetic weakness triggered, and so remain celiacs for life.

Other Autoimmune Diseases

If I'm right in my presumption, then this may also have implications for other autoimmune diseases. One of my cousins (I have a big extended family) recently died from Multiple Sclerosis (MS). I had tried to stay current with research on the disease to see if I could spot potential treatments that could help. One of the more controversial studies done on MS indicated that it might be caused by a bacterial infection, much like stomach ulcers, and could be treated with antibiotics. This never gained widespread

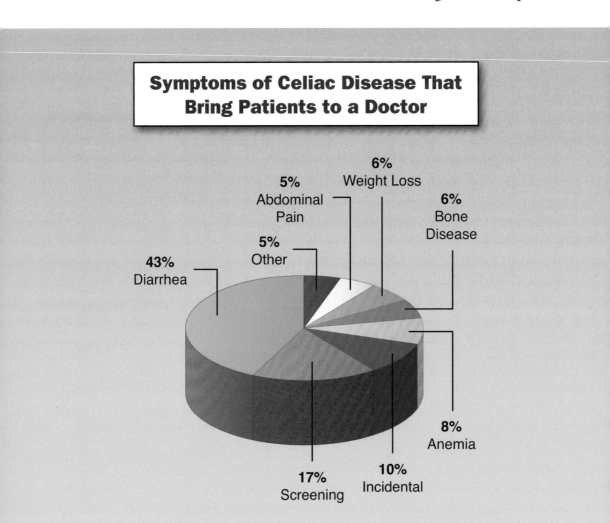

Symptoms of Celiac Disease That Bring Patients to a Doctor

6% Weight Loss

5% Abdominal Pain

6% Bone Disease

5% Other

43% Diarrhea

8% Anemia

17% Screening

10% Incidental

Taken from: R.A. Pagan et al. eds., "Celiac Disease," *Gene Reviews*, University of Washington–Seattle/National Institutes of Health. www.ncbi.nlm.nih.gov/books/NGK1727.

acceptance among researchers, but suppose the study was half-right? Suppose that MS was triggered by a bacterial infection? Indeed, suppose this is the explanation for many or all autoimmune diseases, where the body attacks itself, triggered by some external factor? It would cause us to radically rethink how to approach these diseases, including serious consideration of gene therapy to un-trigger the genetic susceptibility (if that's possible) and cure celiac disease—as well as Crohn's, MS, and all the other autoimmunes.

As I've said, this is speculation on my part, but it's the only explanation I've heard that makes sense to me and accounts for all I've observed. I don't think that the widespread and seemingly accelerating celiac pandemic is adequately explained by greater awareness alone. Something else is at work, and seems to be spreading fast. And since we have no idea what it is, no defense is possible.

Meanwhile, the pizza, pastry, and cake industries should be afraid, very afraid.

It Is Likely That the Celiac Disease Epidemic Is Caused by Environmental Factors

Elaine Fawcett

In the following viewpoint, Elaine Fawcett contends that modern living has caused an epidemic of celiac disease. According to Fawcett, modern humans ingest, breathe, or absorb a sea of toxins every day. It is these toxins, along with a sugar-laden, high-carbohydrate diet and hybridized wheat, that are causing a dramatic increase in the prevalence of celiac disease and other autoimmune disorders, she says.

Fawcett is a nutritional therapy practitioner, health writer, and creator of the website elainefawcett.com.

Celiac disease made national news this summer [July 2009] when a study revealed the disease is four times more common now than it was in the 1950s. Researchers at the Mayo Clinic analyzed frozen blood samples from Air Force personnel collected between 1948 and 1954, and compared them to recent samples. Not only was the rate of celiac disease in the modern subjects more than four times higher, but the rate of death among the Air Force personnel with undiagnosed celiac disease was also four times higher than those who tested negative. In other words, the researchers concluded, "silent" celiac disease quadruples your risk of death.

The fact that a major newswire [Reuters] picked up the story means the gluten-free diet is rapidly losing its association with the zealous and the sickly. As gluten intolerance goes mainstream, it opens the doorway for the nutritional therapy practitioner to educate a newly opened mind. Who knew Grandma could ever be open to information about a gluten-free diet after reading the news online? It's important to be armed with a few facts when questions or misconceptions about celiac disease arise.

The average person thinks celiac disease is a modern malady, but in fact it's quite ancient. After all, the word celiac was coined by a Greek physician in the second century AD, and has piqued medical interest on and off throughout the centuries, especially in the last decade. Celiac disease really began with the introduction of grain as humans transitioned from a hunter-gatherer diet to an agricultural diet, experiencing an increase in disease as a result.

As nutritional researcher Weston Price DDS, discovered in his world travels, early humans mitigated the deleterious effects of gluten by rendering the grain more digestible through sprouting and fermenting it. Also, our ancestors most likely could better tolerate this ancient grain when properly prepared, as they did not weather nearly the immune burdens we do today.

The Rise in Celiac Disease

Today, however, we cannot get through one day without enduring some assault to our physiology, whether it is environmental, dietary or stress-related. It's no wonder that an already compromised food, such as a gluten, can so easily become the proverbial straw that breaks the camel's back.

When pondering the four-fold increase of celiac disease in the last 50 years, it's important to remember that it is an autoimmune disease, and that autoimmune diseases have mushroomed in recent years. As Donna Jackson Nakazawa illustrates in her book *The Autoimmune Epidemic*, top medical journals have reported rising rates of numerous autoimmune diseases around the world in the last 15 years. Rates of Type I diabetes have increased fivefold in the last 40 years, and for children 4 and under, it's increasing 6 percent a year. It's estimated one in five people in the United States suffer from an autoimmune disease, the majority of them women.

A Sea of Toxins

Nakazawa presciently shuns the media's attraction to the "hygiene hypothesis," the pat notion that we are getting sicker because we are too clean, as a cause for autoimmune disease—true to form, the Reuters story jumped right to this explanation. Instead she points to the sea of toxins that we breathe, ingest and absorb every day.

FAST FACT

Scientists estimate that 1 percent of the population worldwide (nearly 68 million people in 2011) is affected by celiac disease.

In random samplings researchers have found more than 100 highly toxic chemicals in people's blood and urine, and 287 pollutants in the fetal-cord blood of newborns. Studies show that mice and rats subjected to low but chronic levels of environmental toxins are more likely to develop autoimmune diseases and impaired immune development. Worst affected are people working directly with pesticides, textiles, solvents, benzene, asbestos and other toxic compounds, as they are more likely to develop and die from autoimmune diseases than those who don't.

Add to this the myriad and numerous chemicals that can be found on virtually every box, bag, bottle and tub in your local grocery store; invisible but ever present elec-

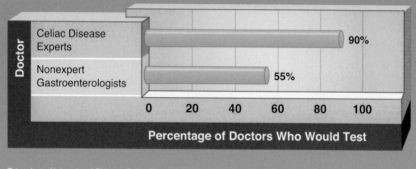

Doctors Do Not Always Check for Celiac Disease

Based on a worldwide survey of gastroenterologists, these figures show the approximate average percentages of doctors who would test for celiac disease in a patient who presented with symptoms such as iron-deficient anemia, delayed puberty, unexplained infertility, or elevated liver enzymes.

Doctor

Celiac Disease Experts — 90%

Nonexpert Gastroenterologists — 55%

0   20   40   60   80   100

Percentage of Doctors Who Would Test

Taken from: University of Chicago Celiac Disease Center, "How Good Are Gastroenterologists at Diagnosing and Treating Celiac Disease?," June 2010.

tromagnetic frequencies, the stress of being a modern American—and it becomes obvious we are overburdened. "Rising levels of autoimmune disease may well prove to be the next environmental disaster," writes Nakazawa in a *Washington Post* story. "Only in this case, the changes taking place degree by degree are in the interior landscapes of our bodies."

One would think, given the statistics and the fact that our children are most grievously affected (Hello? Autism?), that the public health response would be equally significant. Autoimmune diseases affect about 24 million people. However, as Nakazawa shows, the National Institutes of Health [NIH] spent $591 million in autoimmune research in 2003, compared to $5 billion in research for cancer, which affects 9 million people. Likewise, the NIH budget for cardiovascular disease, which affects 22 million, is four times that of autoimmune disease.

Exposure to everyday household chemicals may contribute to the frequency of autoimmune diseases. (© Independent Picture Service/Alamy)

Celiac Disease and Sugar

As detailed in the new book *Why Do I Still Have Thyroid Symptoms When My Lab Tests Are Normal?* by Datis Kharrazian, the sugar-laden, high-carbohydrate diet is another instigating factor for autoimmune disease, including celiac disease. A high-carb diet unleashes a relentless and rotating barrage of sugar, then insulin, into the bloodstream. This keeps the body in a state of alarm, slowly eroding hormonal balance, rapidly degenerating brain tissue, creating nutritional deficiencies, causing gut infections and severely weakening and dysregulating the immune system. In other words, it's a perfect set up for developing an autoimmune disease.

Another consequence of the high-carb diet is the risk for developing candida overgrowth, a yeast infection of the body. Research has shown protein sequences in candida cells and gliadin (the offending part of gluten) are virtually identical, and that a candida overgrowth can trigger celiac disease.

The Way Wheat Was

Also guilty of triggering celiac disease or a gluten intolerance is wheat itself, and, more importantly, what's become of it over the years. The wheat our ancestors ate was a radically different grain compared to what Americans consume today. It has long been hybridized, especially during the last 50 years, to increase yields, cultivation and performance, but not digestion or nutritional value. Spurred on by the grain-based USDA [US Department of Agriculture] Food Pyramid, wheat is also government subsidized. This makes it cheap and therefore a popular ingredient in virtually every processed food on the shelves (although the growing popularity of gluten-free foods is slowly changing that). Add to that the way wheat is stored in the United States—in large silos for long periods of time where molds and fungi grow, and you have yet another potential trigger for autoimmune disease. Studies are increasingly showing a link between gluten (and, in some studies, casein) and autoimmune disease, particularly [the thyroid disorder] Hashimoto's disease. . . .

You Teach, You Teach, You Teach

With the Reuters story hitting the mainstream, as well as the release of a new book about celiac disease by *View* host Elisabeth Hasselbeck, "gluten-free diet" is destined to become a household term. Researchers are already fast at work developing a pharmaceutical drug that would allow persons with celiac disease to safely eat gluten. This might be good news for the acutely sensitive celiac sufferer, but as usual, it's attempting to repair the hole in the dike with a band aid.

Celiac disease and gluten intolerance are not the disease so much as the symptoms of a larger disease affecting us all, even those who enjoy their whole wheat toast with nary a symptom. One person gets celiac disease, while the next contracts a debilitating autoimmune condition that causes paralysis. In the end, such autoimmune maladies are warning flags that we are creating a world and a way of life less able to support human life with every passing day. Gluten intolerance is simply a metaphor for an intolerance of a civilization that was built on the cultivation of wheat. And think about autoimmune disease: It is the body attacking and destroying the self. Is that not an apt metaphor for our relationship to the planet?

It's no use stressing out about our predicament. After all, stress is the most potent toxin of them all, and anyone with an autoimmune condition will tell you it gets worse when they're under a lot of stress. But if we wish to find peace from the environmental disaster that plagues the inner landscape of so many, then it's important to keep celiac disease and other autoimmune diseases in perspective—they are reflections of the planet, telling their story through our bodies.

Celiac Disease Screening May Be Cost Effective

Tiberiu Hershcovici, Moshe Leshno, Eran Goldin, Raanan Shamir, and Eran Israeli

According to scientists from various Israeli university medical centers, it may be cost effective to screen young adults for celiac disease. The scientists—Tiberiu Hershcovici, Moshe Leshno, Eran Goldin, Raanan Shamir, and Eran Israeli—used a statistical modeling program to estimate the cost effectiveness of a celiac disease screening program for healthy eighteen-year-olds. Because a delay between the presentation of symptoms and the diagnosis of celiac disease can be significant (and health care and other costs in the interim can be substantial), and because the gluten-free diet is an effective treatment, their model indicated that screening the general population for the disease would be cost-effective and beneficial. Hershcovici, Goldin, and Israeli are with the gastroenterology unit at Hadassah–Hebrew University Medical Center. Leshno is with Tel Aviv University, and Shamir is with Tel Aviv University and Schneider Children's Medical Center of Israel.

SOURCE: Tiberiu Hershcovici, Moshe Leshno, Eran Goldin, Raanan Shamir, and Eran Israeli, excerpted from "Cost Effectiveness of Mass Screening for Coeliac Disease Is Determined by Time-Delay to Diagnosis and Quality of Life on a Gluten-Free Diet," *Alimentary Pharmacology & Therapeutics,* April 2010, pp. 902–907. Indianapolis, IN: Wiley. Copyright © 2010 by Wiley Publishing, Inc. All rights reserved. Reproduced by permission. http://onlinelibrary.wiley.com /doi/10.1111/j.1365-2036.2010.04242.x/abstract.

Coeliac [celiac] disease (CD) is a gluten-sensitive enteropathy [intestinal disease] with large negative health consequences. CD can appear at any age, and has lately emerged as a worldwide public health problem. The disease is triggered by ingestion of the gluten proteins contained in wheat, barley, and rye, and symptoms range from minor complaints to severe symptomatic presentation. An overall increased morbidity and mortality have been reported in adults with CD. Gluten-free diet (GFD), the only treatment currently available for CD, involves lifelong elimination of the causative prolamines [plant proteins] from the diet.

A majority of CD patients are now initially diagnosed by highly sensitive and specific serological [blood] tests, followed by readily performed endoscopic biopsy. Consequently, many more patients with only mild clinical symptoms are diagnosed, making the classical scenario of diarrhoea/steatorrhoea [fat in stool] and weight loss a comparative rarity.

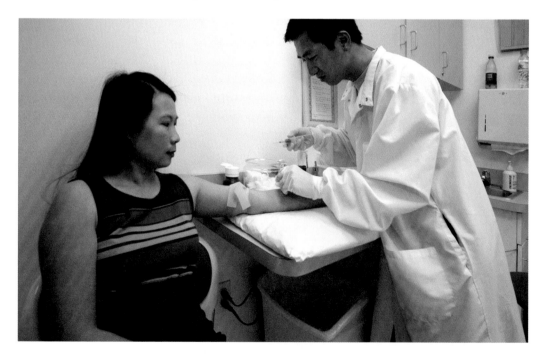

A majority of celiac patients are currently diagnosed by undergoing highly sensitive and specific blood tests, followed by endoscopic biopsy. (© Spencer Grant/Photo Researchers, Inc.)

Theoretically, there are many points favouring mass screening in CD: it is a common disorder that causes significant health problems with an effective treatment available, which results in symptomatic relief and also prevents the complications of the disease. To consider whether mass screening is justified, its impact on quality of life and its cost-effectiveness (CE) must be considered. An NIH [National Institutes of Health] consensus statement published in 2005, as well as a recent debate in this subject referred to the paucity of data on the CE of screening.

The robustness of a CE analysis can be measured in sensitivity analyses [a statistical model that analyzes uncertainty] where some or all of the parameters are varied within a plausible range. The aim of the present study was to define the parameters which have the highest impact on the CE of mass screening of the young adult population for CD. We calculated the cut-off values of these parameters that would allow maintaining the CE of the screening strategy.

Analyzing Cost-Effectiveness

We developed a state transition Markov model [a statistical model used in health care to analyze the cost-effectiveness of different policies related to chronic diseases] to study the effect of different parameters on the CE of screening. The target population is young adults from the entire general population at the age of 18 years. The time horizon of this analysis is the life time. All patients were followed up until death. As the model uses values that can vary between studies and countries, the effect of establishing a certain value on the model was examined using sensitivity analysis. Persons were placed into one of the following health states in each cycle of the model:

(i) No CD;
(ii) CD undiagnosed but with symptoms: Irritable Bowel Syndrome (IBS)-like symptoms, iron-deficiency anaemia (IDA) or other symptoms;
(iii) CD undiagnosed without symptoms;

 (iv) CD diagnosed and adherence to a GFD;

 (v) CD diagnosed without adherence to a GFD;

(vi) Death.

In our model, with its cycle length of 1 year, we evaluated the following screening strategy: determination of human IgA [immunoglobulin-A] anti-tissue transglutaminase antibodies (IgA anti-tTG). In subjects with a positive serology, confirmation of the diagnosis was done by intestinal biopsy. In IgA-deficient patients, human IgG anti-tTG was used. We compared the screening strategy to a 'no-screening' strategy (in which coeliac disease is diagnosed based on symptoms of the subjects).

As guidelines on economic analyses suggest that QALYs [Quality Adjusted Life Years; a measure of quality and quantity of life lived] are the most appropriate unit for a CE analysis, we measured the efficacy by this parameter. We calculated the incremental cost effectiveness ratio (ICER) between the screening and the 'no-screening' strategy. . . .

How Screening Is Cost Effective

Screening for CD is advocated by current guidelines only in high risk groups with conditions associated with an increase in CD prevalence. CE of targeted screening for high risk groups has been shown in subjects with IBS and with Down's syndrome. We developed a state transition Markov model to evaluate the effect of different parameters on the CE of screening vs. no-screening strategy for CD of the young adult general population.

The time delay from onset of symptoms to diagnosis of CD in the no-screening arm was found to be the most important independent determinant of the CE. Although this finding could have been intuitive, our model enabled us to calculate the cut-off values of this parameter and its interaction with other parameters on CE. Various investigators have noted a long duration of symptoms before the diagnosis of CD. In one retro-

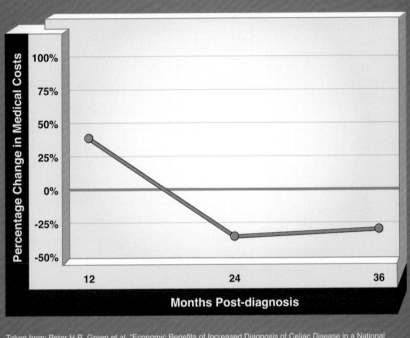

The Diagnosis of Celiac Disease Leads to Reduced Medical Costs, 2001–2003

Taken from: Peter H.R. Green et al. "Economic Benefits of Increased Diagnosis of Celiac Disease in a National Managed Care Population in the United States," *Journal of Insurance Medicine*, June 2008.

spective study from Germany, the interval from onset of symptoms to the first visit to a physician was greatly surpassed by the interval from the first visit to a physician to diagnosis. Thus, the long duration of symptoms was mostly because of a physician delay in reaching the diagnosis rather than a patient delay in seeking medical attention. Although the total time to diagnosis of CD has decreased in the most recent studies, it remains high. The findings of consultations with multiple physicians and a previous diagnosis of IBS in a substantial number of patients suggest that a similar situation exists in the United States. A plausible explanation would be that physicians regard adult CD as rare and fail to consider it in clinical situations other than the classical state of chronic diarrhoea and malabsorption.

The second parameter with a large impact on CE is the utility of treated CD. In our analysis, we used data from a study on Swedish CD patients adhering to a GFD. This was the only study found in the systematic literature review that directly measured the quality of life of treated CD. Although adult CD patients on long-term GFD experienced more gastrointestinal symptoms than the general population, the utility of treated CD in this study was relatively high. It is also reasonable to assume that there would be a strong cultural effect on the utility of adherence to a GFD. . . .

Possible shortcomings of the present model should be noted. First, there are no studies that directly compare the impact of a GFD on the quality of life of asymptomatic CD patients. This question must be addressed by future clinical studies. . . .

Our model allowed us to identify the crucial parameters that play a role in the CE of mass screening. Not less important is defining which parameters do not significantly impact the model within a wide range of values used in the sensitivity analyses. Thus, policy makers can decide on mass screening for CD in a certain society or certain geographical area, on the basis of local values of these parameters. When the time to diagnosis from initiation of symptoms compatible with CD is less than 6 years, our model predicts lack of CE of mass-screening. Thus, education of health professionals to increased awareness for CD diagnosis in symptomatic individuals (thereby decreasing the time-delay to diagnosis) may be a valid alternative to screening. High-quality studies directly examining the utility of screening-diagnosed CD are needed to validate our base-case scenario.

FAST FACT

According to the National Foundation for Celiac Awareness, five thousand to twelve thousand dollars is the average cost of misdiagnosis of celiac per person/per year, not including lost work time.

The Harms of Celiac Disease Screening Outweigh the Benefits

Pekka Collin

In the following viewpoint, Pekka Collin asserts that mass screening for celiac disease is not justified. Collin says that there are many points favoring mass screening for celiac disease, such as easy-to-perform tests and the availability of an effective treatment—the gluten-free diet. However, he says, identifying asymptomatic individuals (those who have celiac disease but do not have symptoms) would cause harm to their perceived quality of life as they may struggle with the restrictions of a gluten-free diet. Collin says since the risks of developing cancer and other long-term complications of celiac disease are low for asymptomatic individuals, mass screening to identify them would be more harmful than beneficial.

Collin is a scientist at Tampere University Hospital and Medical School in Tampere, Finland.

SOURCE: Pekka Collin, "Should Adults Be Screened for Celiac Disease? What Are the Benefits and Harms of Screening?," *Gastroenterology*, April 2005, pp. S104–S108. Oxford, England: Elsevier Science Publishers BV.

Celiac disease is an immune-mediated condition in which ingestion of dietary gluten results in small intestinal mucosal inflammation, crypt hyperplasia, and villous atrophy [i.e., intestinal damage] in genetically susceptible individuals. Typical symptoms in adults are diarrhea, loss of weight, abdominal discomfort, bloating, and various types of malabsorption. The classic symptoms as described in textbooks at this time constitute only a minor subgroup of patients with gluten sensitivity, and many patients present with only subtle or no symptoms. The symptoms may also be atypical and appear outside the gastrointestinal tract. The search for celiac disease in subjects having unequivocal symptoms and signs of the disease is challenging. The widespread use of serologic [blood] screening methods could potentially help to reduce the "celiac iceberg" effect [an image used to explain that those diagnosed with celiac represent a small number of those afflicted with the disease]. Screening programs could include unselected populations, patients with a clinical suspicion of celiac disease, or patients known to be at risk of the condition.

Many Factors Favor Mass Screening

In large population-based screening programs, useful tests must be easy to perform on large numbers of individuals. The disease to be screened must be a common disorder that causes an important health problem. Finally, an effective treatment of the disease must be available; the treatment should result in symptomatic relief and also prevent the complications of the disease. Thus, theoretically, there are many points favoring mass screening in celiac disease.

Antireticulin and antigliadin antibodies were the first tests to be used in screening. The benefits of the IgA-class antiendomysial and the more recent anti-tissue transglutaminase tests are obvious. They offer a sensitivity of 85%–100% and 95%–100%, and a specificity of

95%–100% and 94%–100%, respectively. The anti-tissue transglutaminase test, based on enzyme-linked immunosorbent assay test, is easier to perform and less observer dependent and is therefore more suitable for large screening programs than the antiendomysial test.

Screening studies in different populations have shown that the prevalence of the disease is much higher than previously thought, 1% or more in both the United States and Europe. The prevalence of detected cases is much lower, from 0.27% to 0.02%. This means that, for every patient with the diagnosis of celiac disease, 3–10 remain undetected. The symptoms are diverse, and the disease may be symptom free; it is therefore apparent that, without active serologic screening, the majority of celiac cases will remain undiagnosed in the future.

Untreated celiac disease predisposes individuals to several complications. Abdominal symptoms, anemia, osteopenia, and severe malabsorption can obviously be prevented by early diagnosis and gluten-free dietary treatment. The risk of small intestinal lymphoma [cancer] is increased in celiac disease, and dietary treatment has been shown to prevent the development of malignancy. Similarly, the mortality in untreated celiac disease exceeds that in the population in general, which seems not to be the case in adequately treated individuals. The obvious reason for the increased mortality is the occurrence of small intestinal lymphoma.

It has been hypothesized that gluten would be directly involved in the pathogenesis of autoimmune conditions in genetically susceptible individuals, and autoimmune development might be prevented with an early commencement of gluten-free diet. [A study by Alessandro] Ventura et al. showed that, when adolescents with celiac disease had adopted a gluten-free diet in early childhood,

FAST FACT

According to Alessio Fasano from the University of Maryland Center for Celiac Research, 95 percent of people with celiac disease are undiagnosed or misdiagnosed with other conditions.

Lymphoma, or cancer of the intestine, is shown here. Untreated celiac disease can lead to intestinal lymphomas. (© Gastrolab/Photo Researchers, Inc.)

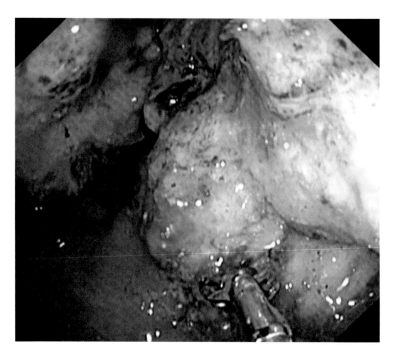

the number of autoimmune conditions was lower than in patients in whom the treatment had been introduced later in life. The hypothesis is still debatable: On the contrary, it has been suggested that it is the age of the patients and not the duration of gluten exposure that predicts the occurrence of autoimmune conditions.

Considering the Impact on Quality of Life for Symptom-Free Celiacs

The crucial questions in considering population screening are whether we are doing more harm than benefit, and what are the costs of the approach? The benefits of early diagnosis of celiac disease seem to be obvious. However, most studies have been carried out in symptomatic and clinically detected celiac disease patients. The natural history of symptom-free or screen-detected disease is less well understood.

To answer the question of whether mass screening is justified, its impact on quality of life must be considered.

Health-related quality of life takes into account, apart from the physical, also the social and emotional aspects of well-being. It appears that adults with newly detected celiac disease gain substantial improvement in health-related quality of life within the first year of treatment with a gluten-free diet. However, evidence suggests that the long-term effects are less satisfactory. [C.] Hallert et al. showed that the burden of disease was worse in female celiac disease patients who had been on a gluten-free diet for 10 years than in age-matched female controls. Similarly, long-term-treated adults with celiac disease, again especially female patients, experienced significantly more gastrointestinal symptoms than controls. Male and female celiac disease patients may cope differently with the everyday dietary restrictions, which might explain the sex difference in perceived well-being.

In the study of [Kirsi] Mustalahti et al., quality of life was significantly better in 19 screen-detected than in 21 symptom-detected celiac patients before the treatment. After 1 year on a gluten-free diet, quality of life improved in screen-detected subjects and seemed to be actually better than that in controls without celiac disease. It is possible, however, that the observed improvement would be only temporary; the long-term impact of diet on quality of life in apparently symptom-free patients is subject to further studies. An additional concern is the poor long-term adherence to the gluten-free diet, even in symptom detected patients: According to some studies, only 45%–65% were following a strict gluten-free diet. The compliance might be even worse in screen-detected patients. In the study of [Elizabetta] Fabiani et al., only 5 of 22 patients with celiac disease, diagnosed by means of serologic screening, were maintaining a strict gluten-free diet after 5 years of treatment.

The poor compliance in screen-detected individuals may jeopardize many conceivable advantageous effects of the mass screening. When asymptomatic patients are encouraged to withdraw gluten from their diet lifelong, this may increase the burden of disease and impair quality of life.

Low Risks for Symptom-Free Patients

Most screen-detected patients with celiac disease do not have apparent symptoms. What is their lifetime risk of serious or significant complications of celiac disease, provided that they remain undetected?

The risk of small intestinal lymphoma has earlier been reported to be 50–100-fold compared with the population in general. This notwithstanding, it is not known whether active population screening would reduce the development of malignancy or mortality. In earlier studies, only a minority of celiac patients had been detected and treated, and the overall risk of malignancy is thus lower than previously thought.

It is debatable whether patients with silent celiac disease have any increased risk of lymphoma. Provided that celiac disease would be a major etiologic [causal] factor in the development of lymphoma, one would also expect to detect many silent cases in patients suffering from lymphoma. Some recent screening studies have addressed this issue. [Carlo] Catassi et al. found celiac disease in 6 (0.92%) of 653 patients with non-Hodgkin lymphoma. Another study from Italy reported 1 (1.25%) of 80 patients with non-Hodgkin lymphoma to suffer from celiac disease. Similarly, in Spain, the overall risk of celiac disease in patients suffering from non-Hodgkin lymphoma was low, only 0.67% (2 of 298). These results indicate that untreated symptom-free celiac disease is not a major factor in the development of non-Hodgkin lymphoma.

It has been found in many studies that low bone mineral density is a common complication of celiac disease. Evidence shows that osteopenia and osteoporosis are alleviated on a gluten-free diet, although not completely in

Assumed Beneficial and Harmful Effects of Mass Screening for Celiac Disease

	Population screening
Early detection of celiac disease	Beneficial
Specific treatment available	Beneficial
Dietary compliance adequate after diagnosis	Questionable
Prevention of complications	Questionable
Improvement in quality of life	May be harmful

Taken from: Pekka Collin, "Should Adults Be Screened for Celiac Disease? What Are the Benefits and Harms of Screening?," *Gastroenterology*, April 2005.

adults. Small studies from Finland and France indicate that the bone mineral density would be reduced also in adults with symptom-free untreated celiac disease. The clinical importance of the reduction of bone mineral density is the increased risk of fractures. [Horatio] Vazquez et al. observed that patients with celiac disease seem to have experienced more fractures than nonceliac disease controls. By contrast, [K.] Thomason et al. demonstrated only a small and nonsignificant increase in fracture risk in celiac disease patients. A large population-based cohort study in the United Kingdom, comprising 4732 subjects with celiac disease and 23,620 matched controls, showed that the overall hazard ratio in celiac disease patients for any fracture was 1.30 and for hip fracture, 1.90. These excess risks were statistically significant but, as the authors stated, were at most modest from the clinical point of view. The results of this important study, therefore, indicate that mass screening for celiac disease is not warranted.

Costs of Screening

Cost-effectiveness and cost-utility studies are necessary before introducing mass screening for celiac disease outside of clinical trials. Such studies are lacking so far. For comparison, testing for celiac disease in patients with irritable bowel syndrome suggested that screening costs would be acceptable when the prevalence of celiac disease is 1.0%–3.4%, and the testing would be the dominant strategy when the prevalence exceeds 8%. These recommendations cannot of course be applied in symptomless patients or in the general population.

A similar decision analysis model showed that testing with anti-tissue transglutaminase antibody test alone achieved most of the clinical benefits with a reasonable cost when comparisons were made with different test panels. In irritable bowel syndrome, the testing proved to be effective, even at relatively low prevalence rates of celiac disease, namely 0.5%–1.0%. The authors emphasized that these results do not advocate mass screening: They measured gains in quality-adjusted life years, and such symptomatic improvement would be unlikely in asymptomatic subjects with celiac disease. In the absence of evidence to the contrary, it is reasonable to assume that celiac screening would be acceptable even when subtle or nonspecific symptoms are present, provided that the estimated prevalence of celiac disease is approximately 4%. . . .

In conclusion, evidence today does not support mass screening of celiac disease. . . . More research is needed to assess the cost-effectiveness benefits of mass screening. The occurrence of osteoporosis and fractures and the possible beneficial effect of a gluten-free diet should be investigated in a large group of symptom-free patients. Dietary compliance and quality of life before and after a gluten-free diet should likewise be evaluated thoroughly. Currently, the best approach is to focus on case finding by screening in individuals known to have an increased risk of celiac disease.

The Gluten-Free Trend Has Health Benefits for All

Jennifer Harshman

In the following viewpoint, Jennifer Harshman contends that a gluten-free diet can be beneficial even for people who do not have celiac disease. Harshman relates that many people believe going gluten-free can help with medical conditions such as fibromyalgia and diabetes. People who have symptoms such as acid reflux, headache, or constipation can also be helped by going gluten-free, she contends. According to Harshman, some people may benefit not just from a gluten-free diet but also from a diet free of casein, a milk protein.

Harshman is a writer who covers medical, psychological, educational, and children's issues.

Celiacs aren't the only ones who should go gluten-free [GF]. The GF Diet, used for weight loss and part of treatment for many medical conditions, is getting easier to follow. Celiac disease diagnosis is one great reason to avoid gluten, but it's certainly not the only reason to follow a gluten-free diet. Gluten intolerance is increasing throughout the world, and millions are discovering that eating wheat and other foods that contain gluten is causing problems for them.

Reasons to Go Gluten-Free

Gluten is a type of protein that Alessio Fasano, M.D., calls "useless" to the human body. At best, it is filler that is taking the place of nutritious food; at worst, it is a poison that is causing the body to self-destruct. Dr. Fasano is Director of the Mucosal Biology Research Center, University of Maryland School of Medicine.

A gluten-free, casein-free [gfcf] diet is often prescribed by Kenneth Bock, M.D., for patients who have autism, ADHD [attention-deficit/hyperactivity disorder], asthma or allergies. In his book, *Healing the New Childhood Epidemics,* he explains that gluten and casein are proteins that cause problems in the body, triggering the immune system. A gfcf diet can help improve symptoms associated with many medical conditions. Examples of conditions that might be helped by the diet are fibromyalgia and diabetes. A gluten-free diet may make it easier to control blood sugar levels, according to Donna Korn in *Living Gluten-Free for Dummies.*

The desire to improve a chronic disease may prompt some to go gluten-free. A gluten-free diet might also help those who haven't been diagnosed with a chronic disease, but are suffering from various symptoms such as headache, constipation, diarrhea, gas, bloating, or acid reflux. Removing gluten from the diet may be enough for some people, but many people will need to remove both gluten and casein from their diet to see improvement in their symptoms. According to "Celiac Disease: Wheat Ails You?" on the American Diabetes Association website, many who have problems with gluten also need to avoid dairy products.

FAST FACT

About 10 percent of people with type 1 diabetes also have celiac disease, according to the American Diabetes Association.

Following a gluten-free, casein-free diet (gfcf diet) can be complicated, but it does not have to be. Increasing numbers of food manufacturers such as Pamela's Products and even Betty Crocker are producing foods that are safe to eat. Substitute foods may be tasty, but are not necessary for a healthy diet.

A simple diet of unprocessed fruits, vegetables, and protein sources such as legumes, fish and meat is naturally gluten-free and casein free. Eating nutritious whole foods is healthier than eating processed foods. If packaged foods are purchased, reading and knowing ingredients on food labels is a must. Milk ingredients and gluten ingredients are hidden in many foods.

A gluten-free diet may help those who, although not suffering from a chronic disease, exhibit such symptoms as headaches, constipation, acid reflux, and others. (© joefoxfoodanddrink/ Alamy)

Consult a Medical Professional Before Going Gluten-Free

Only a medical professional can give medical advice, and it is always best to consult a medical practitioner such as a doctor prior to making any changes in diet or exercise. . . . Going gluten-free before consulting a doctor is not advisable for those who want a medical diagnosis. Some sources, such as the American Diabetes Association article mentioned above, say that trying a gluten-free diet might help

Physicians' Views on Using a Gluten-Free, Casein-Free Diet to Treat Autism

Based on a 2007 survey of 539 American physicians:

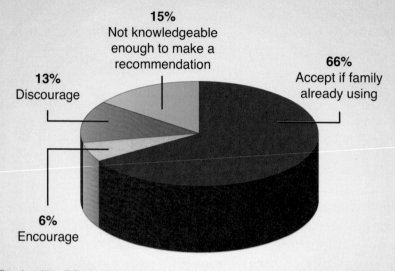

15%
Not knowledgeable
enough to make a
recommendation

66%
Accept if family
already using

13%
Discourage

6%
Encourage

Taken from: Allison E. Golnik and Marjorie Ireland, "Complementary Alternative Medicine for Children with Autism: A Physician Survey," *Journal of Autism and Developmental Disorders*, July 2009.

to convince a doctor (that a patient has celiac disease), but consulting a professional prior to making dietary changes is especially important if celiac disease, wheat allergy, gluten allergy, or gluten intolerance is suspected. Why? Staff at the Mayo Clinic say that cutting gluten and/or casein before being tested can invalidate the medical test results. Antibodies and intestinal damage can only be detected when a person has been eating the offending foods.

When gluten (and/or casein) is removed from the diet, the body will begin to heal, and will cease production of the substances for which the doctors will test. Conceivably, even confirmed celiacs could "pass" the typical screening tests after being on a gluten-free diet. If a medical diagnosis is needed, patients should consult a doctor before making dietary changes in order to avoid interfering with an accurate diagnosis.

There Is No Evidence That a Gluten-Free Diet Offers Benefits for All

Ayala Laufer-Cahana

In the following viewpoint, Ayala Laufer-Cahana contends that the gluten-free diet has become a fad that is being touted as a treatment for all kinds of medical disorders. According to Laufer-Cahana, there are only two established medical reasons to go on a gluten-free diet: to treat celiac disease or the skin condition dermatitis herpetiformis. There is no evidence that going gluten-free helps people with other conditions, such as autism or those trying to lose weight, she maintains.

Laufer-Cahana is a physician specializing in pediatrics and medical genetics and is the cofounder of the company Herbal Water Inc.

Have you noticed the gluten-free food explosion? I have the privilege of attending many food shows, and I'm stunned by the proliferation of grain based foods—prepared meals, cookies, snacks bread and crackers—developed for the benefit of those on a gluten-free diet and with "gluten-free" as a marketing proposition.

Gluten-free foods are a necessity for people with celiac disease, a disorder resulting from an immune reaction to gluten. But are these foods good for everyone else? While the precise prevalence of celiac disease isn't known, it's estimated to range from about 0.4 percent to about one percent of the general population in the U.S. (up to three million Americans). The number of Americans with *physician-diagnosed celiac,* however, although growing, is still not very large, and estimated anywhere in the range of 40,000–110,000 cases.

Not to sound cynical, but even a one percent consumer base wouldn't drive manufacturers and retailers to the accelerated expansion of the gluten-free options we're seeing. The reason food manufacturers have jumped in full force into this market is because gluten-free products are now favored not only by celiac patients, but by many people *without* the diagnosis—gluten free is indeed the latest food fad—and it's a huge opportunity to make money. Research firm Mintel estimates that nearly 10 percent of shoppers currently seek gluten-free foods; they forecast 15–25 percent growth in gluten-free product sales in coming years.

FAST FACT

According to research, for patients with celiac disease, daily consumption of fifty milligrams of gluten, equivalent to that contained in one one-hundredth of a slice of standard wheat bread, is damaging to the small intestine.

A Worrisome Fad

I'm glad to see the growing awareness of celiac, and also happy to see that keeping a gluten-free diet is becoming easier, more acceptable, and requires less sacrifice on taste. On the other hand, the "fad" aspect of the gluten-free boom worries me quite a bit. Gluten is a protein found in wheat or related grains. It's a remarkably large molecule that's quite central to the structure and texture of dough.

Gluten is definitely not an evil food component for those not afflicted by celiac. Gluten is part of whole-wheat flours and whole wheat, barley and rye grains—parts of a healthy diet. Although many junk foods contain gluten, gluten isn't what makes these foods not nutritious—it's the other ingredients or the processing of the grains that makes them so. If going gluten-free means choosing from the gluten-free menu at Wendy's or Dairy Queen, or replacing wheat based snacks with corn based ones, you haven't done yourself much good.

There are only two established medical reasons to avoid gluten: celiac disease and dermatitis herpetiformis, a very itchy chronic skin rash of bumps and blisters, frequently linked to celiac. In celiac disease, complete removal of gluten from the diet is necessary for life, and results in complete resolution of symptoms. Non-adherence to a gluten-free diet can have dire consequences (even if the

Those on Gluten-Free Diets May Risk Vitamin B Deficiencies

Many gluten-free grains contain smaller amounts of B vitamins than enriched wheat does. The table below shows the amount in milligrams (mg) of thiamin, riboflavin, niacin, and folate found in 100 grams (g) of various grains.

Grain (100g)	Thiamin (mg)	Riboflavin (mg)	Niacin (mg)	Folate (mg)
Wheat, enriched, containing gluten	0.8	0.5	5.9	183
Gluten-free				
Amaranth, uncooked	0.1	0.2	0.9	82
Millet	0.4	0.3	4.7	85
Potato flour	0.2	0.1	3.5	25
Tapioca	0.0	0.0	0.0	4
Brown rice flour	0.4	0.1	6.3	16

Taken from: Midge Kirby and Elaine Danner, "Nutritional Deficiencies in Children on Restricted Diets," *Pediatric Clinics of North America*, October 2009.

According to the author, there are only two accepted medical reasons to follow a gluten-free diet: to treat celiac disease or dermatitis herpetiformis.
(© Washington Post/ Getty Images)

person is asymptomatic), including poor growth, infertility, osteoporosis, anemia, bowel narrowing and bowel cancer.

A gluten-free diet is now touted for many other conditions, from autism to attention-deficit disorder, irritated bowel syndrome, multiple sclerosis and now even weight loss. Although there are *anecdotal* stories about gluten-free diets making a difference for these conditions, there's really no good evidence to support such advice.

No Evidence of Benefit

The gluten-free casein (milk protein)-free diet is a very common treatment attempt for autism. A Cochrane review did an extensive literature search to identify randomized controlled studies of gluten-free or casein-free diets as an intervention in autistic features. They found only two small randomized controlled studies, with a total of 35 patients between them. The results of one of these studies indicated that a combined gluten- and casein-free diet reduced autistic behavior, but the second study showed no significant difference in outcome measures between the diet group and the control group. The researchers concluded (*emphasis is mine*): "Research has shown high rates of use of complementary and alternative therapies (CAM) for children with autism including gluten and/or casein exclusion diets. *Current evidence for efficacy of these diets is poor.* Large scale, good quality randomised controlled trials are needed."

There's no logical reason why adopting a gluten-free regimen should result in weight loss. Unless you have a strategy of reducing caloric intake on what just happens to be a gluten-free regimen, I can't see how gluten-free for weight reduction makes any sense. In fact, patients with celiac often *gain* weight once they start a gluten-free regimen. The reason is that while they're eating gluten, many suffer abdominal pain, malabsorption and other symptoms that lead to reduced consumption or utilization of food. Once they're on the gluten-free diet they thrive, eat well and gain weight. Perhaps paying more attention to food—no matter what the regimen—can *anecdotally* lead to weight loss, but *there's nothing inherently low calorie or healthy about a gluten-free diet.*

I learned from nutritionist Janet Helm about Elisabeth Hasselbeck's book "*The G Free Diet,*" which Janet criticizes for inaccuracies, and also for "glorifying gluten-free and making it appear to be the best thing since, um, sliced bread."

In the introduction to her book, Hasselbeck (who has celiac disease, and therefore greatly benefited from going gluten-free) writes:

> But a gluten-free lifestyle can help countless others as well. People suffering from a wide range of diseases—from autism to osteoporosis, from diabetes to rheumatoid arthritis— can often benefit from this change in diet. Even people with no health issues have a great deal to gain by giving up gluten. The G-free diet can help with weight management. It can elevate your energy levels, improve your attention span, and speed up your digestion.

To which all I have to say is: Show us the proof! I searched Medline (the online computer database for bio-medical journals) and couldn't find it.

A Clear Standard Must Be Established for Gluten-Free Food Labeling

Christine Boyd

In the following viewpoint, Christine Boyd argues for the establishment of federal guidelines regulating the uses of "gluten-free" labeling. According to Boyd, without a clear federal definition of "gluten-free," the marketplace for celiac disease sufferers is confusing and risky. They are left to wonder whether labels such as "gluten-free," "no gluten," or "without gluten" are valid. Additionally, says Boyd, there is no regulatory mechanism to force manufacturers to recall food inaccurately labeled as gluten-free. Boyd says the US Food and Drug Administration (FDA) was supposed to issue labeling regulations governing gluten-free foods in 2008; however, the agency's rule-making proceedings have been stalled for the last few years. According to Boyd, the FDA must act to define what "gluten-free" really means and restore accountability to the "gluten-free" claim.

Boyd is a medical writer for *Living Without*, a magazine for people with celiac disease and food allergies. She also suffers from celiac disease.

In late 2008, a newspaper investigation revealed that certain gluten-free products manufactured by Wellshire Farms and specifically marketed to children were mislabeled. As news spread about the faulty designation, parents of food allergic kids became furious—and scared. At least two children with wheat allergies developed anaphylaxis to the mislabeled food and required hospitalization. In addition, countless children with celiac disease were sickened, including 2-year-old James Fourie.

"We had just started him on the gluten-free diet," explains James' mom, Stephanie Fourie of Boulder, Colorado. "I cook a lot from scratch but I also rely on packaged foods from time to time, especially when I was first learning the gluten-free diet."

Fourie had purchased mislabeled chicken bites and given them to James. Within an hour or two, his behavior changed, explains Fourie. He crouched down in a corner of his room and was saying something but he was too young to verbalize how he was feeling. From his body language, it looked like he was having severe stomach cramps. Trusting the product was properly labeled, it didn't cross Fourie's mind that the chicken bites were to blame for her son's symptoms. When she offered them to James at a second meal, he refused them. At the time, it was frustrating.

"The chicken bites weren't cheap and I didn't want to make several different things for dinner," says Fourie, who has two other small children. When she read the newspaper report that Wellshire Kids Gluten Free Dinosaur Shapes Chicken Bites, Chicken Corn Dogs and Beef Corn Dogs contained up to 2,200 parts per million of gluten—more than 100 times what celiac experts generally view as acceptable—it was like a light bulb went off. That was why James had mysteriously fallen ill!

Fourie was outraged. She immediately contacted the store where she bought the chicken bites and told them about the mislabeling. But without an official product recall, the store would not pull the products from its shelves. "It was so upsetting," Fourie recalls. "I couldn't stop thinking about all the other parents out there who hadn't read the newspaper story and were feeding their kids these mislabeled products that were making them sick. Who knows how many kids may have had reactions to the mislabeled food? I was so disappointed that no one was doing anything about it."

Wellshire Farms has since posted a response to the mislabeling episode on its website. Although the company pointed to contaminated corn batter as the culprit—it's now working with a new batter supplier—Fourie says the experience has made her wary of the gluten-free label. "I've lost a lot of trust," she says.

Cause for Concern

Shortly after the incident with the chicken bites, Fourie began reading up on gluten-free labeling. She was surprised—and frustrated—to learn that currently in the United States, there is no definition for the use of the term "gluten-free" with regard to food labeling. Neither the U.S. Department of Agriculture [USDA], which oversees egg, meat, and poultry products, nor the Food and Drug Administration [FDA], which covers packaged and most other foods, specifically define the term "gluten-free."

Yet both agencies permit gluten-free labeling, as demonstrated by the increasing assortment of gluten-free foods available. The USDA reviews "gluten free" and other so-called health claims on a case-by-case basis—Wellshire Farms reportedly received USDA approval for its chicken bites in 2001—while the FDA allows manufacturers to affix a gluten-free label on FDA-regulated products provided the claim is "truthful and not misleading." Generally, if a food labeled "free" of a substance actually contains that substance, the FDA considers the claim misleading.

GLUTEN FREE

INGREDIENTS: PASTEURIZED CULTURED MILK AND CREAM, SALT, PARSLEY, BASIL, GARLIC, CAROB BEAN AND/OR GUAR ONION, POTASSIUM

There are no clear federal guidelines regulating the labeling of gluten-free foods. (© FoodIngredients/Alamy)

But this line of reasoning falls short with gluten-free claims.

With other "-free" claims, such as sodium-free or calorie-free, free means zero. But with gluten-free foods, there's no way to test for zero gluten. The technology just isn't there yet, says attorney Andrea Levario, executive director of the American Celiac Disease Alliance (ACDA).

Instead, extremely small quantities—known as parts per million (ppm)—of gluten can be reliably tested. Current analytic techniques can consistently detect 20 ppm of gluten in a variety of foods, including raw, cooked and baked foods. Since celiac experts generally agree that 20 ppm of gluten is a safe threshold for people with celiac disease, many countries have adopted gluten-free standards at or below 20 ppm.

The FDA proposed a less than 20 ppm gluten-free standard in 2006—its first explicit attempt to define the term gluten-free—but the agency has yet to finalize it.

And the USDA is awaiting the FDA's decision before moving ahead on the subject.

With the number of products making unregulated gluten-free claims on the rise, the marketplace can be potentially dangerous for consumers with gluten sensitivity and wheat allergy. And it's no longer just people with celiac disease buying gluten-free foods, notes celiac nutrition expert Shelley Case, RD [registered dietician]. Sales far exceed what the portion of the U.S. population diagnosed with celiac disease might purchase. Consumers are scooping up gluten-free products for reasons that range from weight loss and general health concerns to simple curiosity.

Delayed Regulation

There may be as many as a dozen variations in gluten-free claims, such as "no gluten," "without gluten," "free of gluten," and "no gluten ingredients used." "Is the purity of a product labeled 'no gluten ingredients' the same as one labeled 'gluten free,'" wonders Fourie. "It's very confusing."

She and other consumers aren't the only ones confused. According to a recent FDA report, many food manufacturers would welcome a gluten-free standard to eliminate uncertainty or misunderstanding regarding labeling, as well as to help level the playing field. These companies argue that a standardized definition could assist the industry by promoting fair competition. With a standard in place, all manufacturers would have to adhere to the same labeling requirements.

Why hasn't the FDA finalized its 2006 definition of gluten-free? As part of sweeping legislation known as FALCPA, the Food Allergen Labeling and Consumer Protection Act of 2004, Congress ordered the FDA to define and permit the voluntary use of the term gluten-free on the labeling of foods by August 2008. As directed, the

FDA issued its proposed gluten-free regulation on schedule but has failed to follow through with a final ruling.

While there has been no official explanation for the nearly two-year [now going on four-year] delay, Levario speculates that the voluntary nature of the gluten-free regulation could have something to do with it. Because it's not mandatory, it may not be viewed as an immediate priority, she says. In addition, the 2008 deadline for the final ruling coincided with changing White House administrations. "It might have been a bit of bad timing," Levario says.

In November 2009, the FDA announced plans to conduct an experimental study on gluten-free labeling. The agency hopes the study will gauge public perceptions of various gluten-free claims (e.g., free of gluten, without gluten, no gluten), in addition to related statements (e.g., made in a gluten-free facility, not made in a facility that processes gluten-containing foods). While the study will likely provide the FDA with useful information, Levario advises that it may further delay nailing down a definitive gluten-free standard.

Flimsy Oversight

Without regulation in place, enforcement of gluten-free labeling is feeble at best. "Until the FDA regulations are finalized, it's a question mark at what point the agency would say a product is mislabeled or misleading. Right now, there's no way to know that," says Levario. When gluten-free products have received attention for potential mislabeling in recent years, it's been primarily from consumer groups, not the FDA.

In contrast, when peanut labeling errors have occurred, the FDA requires immediate product recalls. The difference is that there is a labeling standard in place for peanuts, in part because there is an immediate risk to consumers with an allergy, explains Levario. "Someone could die from eating mislabeled peanut products. Gluten doesn't fall into the same risk category."

Estimates of Gluten-Containing Food Consumed in the United States

Age	Consumed per eating occasion	Consumed per day
1 to 18 years	100g	400g
18⁺ years	200g	500g

Grams (g) refer to the weight of food consumed per time period. These estimates reflect the weight of food consumed per time period (per day or per eating occasion) and not the gram weight of gluten consumed.

Taken from: US Food and Drug Administration, Center for Food Safety and Applied Nutrition, "Health Hazard Assessment for Gluten Exposure in Individuals with Celiac Disease," May 2001. Based on the US Department of Agriculture Continuing Survey of Food Intake by Individuals for 1994–1996 and 1998.

While Wellshire Farms may not have been required to issue a recall of its mislabeled products, it could have done so voluntarily. For Fourie, this is hard to swallow. "A recall would have been the responsible thing to do. Mislabeling a product is bad, but failing to recall it is unacceptable," she says. "Companies should want to make the highest quality product. When they issue a recall, it speaks volumes about the company, that they're trying to do the right thing."

A problem with recalls is that many people never hear about them, says Levario. Typically, a recall starts with a press release that's subsequently picked up by various media outlets, blogs and support groups. To stay current, Levario suggests signing up with the Food Allergy and Anaphylaxis Network's (FAAN) special allergy alert listserv at foodallergy.org. FAAN's focus is on product recalls of allergens like milk, eggs, peanuts and soy. Wheat is also covered, but not gluten.

Despite the challenges, considerable progress has been made in product labeling that's been a God-send for food-allergic consumers. FALCPA requires clear identification of the top eight allergens (milk, eggs, tree nuts, peanuts, fish, shellfish, soy and wheat) and Levario points out that the law indirectly benefits those on the gluten-free diet. "Labeling wheat dramatically reduced the label-reading burden for gluten-intolerant consumers," agrees dietician Shelley Case. "The majority of gluten in the North American diet—up to 95 percent of it—comes from wheat."

FALCPA was also a huge step in getting food manufacturers on the side of the food-allergic and food-intolerant community, explains Levario, "We really need to partner with manufacturers and continue to encourage them. Most have been working very hard to comply with the law."

FAST FACT

According to Packaged Facts, US sales of gluten-free products reached more than $2.6 billion by the end of 2010 and are expected to exceed more than $5 billion by 2015.

In fact, many companies started proactively planning for gluten-free regulation as soon as FALCPA passed. Some began researching product-testing protocols from countries with established gluten-free standards. Many looked to Canada, which has had a gluten-free policy in place since 1995. Canada officially defines "gluten-free" as no gluten; however, practically speaking, detection analsyes used put the cut-off for gluten-free foods at 20 ppm.

Internationally, gluten-free labeling standards vary considerably but that may be changing. In 2008, the Codex Alimentarius Commission, which sets international standards for food and food safety, revised its widely referenced gluten-free guideline. Codex now stipulates that gluten-free foods may not contain more than 20 ppm of wheat, rye, barley or oats,[1] a definition comparable to FDA's proposed gluten-free regulation.

1. The 2008 Codex standard allows oats provided they're not cross contaminated with wheat, rye or barley. However, it's up to individual countries to determine how they handle the use of oats.

Certification Programs

While some companies voluntarily observe the less than 20 ppm standard, others have gone further and sought certification from one of several gluten-free certification organizations. In recent years, the Gluten Intolerance Group (GIG), the Celiac Sprue Association (CSA) and the National Foundation for Celiac Awareness (NFCA) have each developed their own certification program to help consumers identify gluten-free foods with more confidence. GIG's program is the Gluten-Free Certification Organization (GFCO). "We modeled GFCO after the top-notch kosher and organic certification programs," says GIG executive director Cynthia Kupper, RD.

To obtain GFCO certification, companies undergo an application process that, according to Kupper, is not a walk in the park. "Making a gluten-free product is different than certifying a product. Companies that apply for GFCO certification are the cream of the crop. They're doing more than they have to," she says. The standard for GFCO-certified products is much stricter than even the proposed FDA standard. GFCO sets 10 ppm as its upper limit. (Once FDA rules on its gluten-free standard, GFCO expects to maintain its 10 ppm limit).

Companies with certification want to win consumer confidence—and they are, reports Kupper. "Consumers used to rely on product lists to identify gluten-free products. Now they're looking for the GFCO stamp. We've grown phenomenally since starting the certification in 2004."

Next to buying certified products, the best safeguard you can take remains reading food labels, says dietician Shelley Case. Because companies can reformulate products or packaging at anytime, reading ingredient labels every time is absolutely paramount for gluten-free consumers, she says. If you're unsure about an ingredient, she recommends contacting the manufacturer directly. If you're unsure about the meaning of a gluten-free claim, she suggests asking the manufacturer questions like these:

- Is the product made in a dedicated gluten-free facility?
- If the product is made in a shared facility (one that produces both gluten-containing and gluten-free foods), is the product made on dedicated equipment?
- What steps does the manufacturer take to prevent cross contamination?
- Does the manufacturer regularly test the final product for gluten? If so, does the product consistently fall below 20 ppm?

Rebuilding Trust

It's been more than a year since Fourie's son, James, ate the mislabeled chicken bites. Happily, he hasn't had any subsequent episodes of painful stomach cramps. "I've been reading labels diligently," reports Fourie. She also seeks out products that bear GFCO certification. "I'm willing to spend a little more on products that have certification. When I need an item that doesn't, I call the company to make sure the final product is tested. If they can't give me an answer I'm comfortable with, we don't eat it." She says she now cooks from scratch more than ever. "Even though it's very time-consuming, I try to provide as many homemade meals and snacks for my children as possible."

Fourie is certain these precautions help keep James healthy. But she worries that a mislabeling fiasco could happen again. "I can take lots of preventative measures but there may be a time when a product is mislabeled and I won't figure it out. To me, it demonstrates the urgency of passing a gluten-free standard." She looks forward to the day when there's accountability behind every gluten-free claim. "That peace of mind will be wonderful," she says.

Editor's note: On August 3, 2011, the FDA announced that it was reopening the rule-making proceedings for "gluten-free" labeling of foods and is prepared to issue final regulations. As of February 2012, it had not issued a ruling.

Foods Containing Oats Should Not Be Labeled "Gluten-Free"

Kinnikinnick Foods, Inc.

In this selection Kinnikinnick Foods, Inc. conveys its opposition to proposed regulations in Canada that would allow oats to be labeled as gluten-free. According to the author, allowing the gluten-free label to apply to oats would be a mistake and would be confusing to consumers. Oats *may* be safe for *most* people with celiac disease, but not for *all* people with celiac disease, the author contends. For those who cannot tolerate oats, the long-term safety impacts could be harmful, so allowing oats to be labeled as gluten-free is not worth the risk, the author maintains.

Kinnikinnick Foods, Inc. is a dedicated gluten-free food manufacturer based in Edmonton, Alberta, Canada.

As is often the case, a question on Twitter this morning [March 25, 2010] has prompted a post. The question was: *"Do you think Kinnikinnick will ever manufacture their own oats for baking & cooking?"* The short answer is No. We won't make, use or sell oats. And that certainly could have been a "tweet" but we get asked this question a lot and it really deserves an in-depth explanation. In order to explain our position, it's probably worth a look at the history of oats, gluten and Celiac Disease.

A Gluten Overview

Let's get right to the basics. What exactly is gluten? The seeds of most flowering plants, especially grains, have evolved to store proteins which provide nourishment during germination. This protein is often called gluten, an unfortunately generic term which in itself causes confusion. The reason for the confusion is that rice and corn contain proteins which are often referred to as rice gluten or corn gluten. These "glutens" are not a concern for people with Celiac as they do not contain the harmful proteins that cause the immune response which is the root of Celiac Disease.

So which "glutens" are the ones people with Celiac need to avoid? For most of the last 50+ years, the grains to avoid have been recognized as Wheat, Barley, Rye and Oats. (WBRO) These grains contain the proteins Gliadin, Horedein, Secalin and Avenin, respectively, and these are the proteins that we really should refer to when we use the word "gluten" in relation to Celiac. However, starting in 1995, some research began to show that some Celiacs were able to tolerate pure, uncontaminated oats. These tests were repeated with varying results over the next 10 years. By around 2005, the consensus began to say that consumption of oats is probably safe for most Celiacs, if intake is limited to around 50–70 g of pure uncontaminated oats, based on a 5-year-long clinical study.

Oats Not Safe for Everyone

Being a family of Celiacs running a company who has been making gluten free foods for almost 20 years, we have some issues, both philosophical and practical, with that premise. Let's look at the philosophical issues first.

It's probably safe for most Celiacs. The problem is that it is certainly not safe for all.

Oats are not recommended within a year of diagnosis because of the [risk of avenin]-sensitive enteropathy. [Wikipedia]

There are case reports of individuals with celiac disease relapsing from the consumption of pure uncontaminated oats. [Mohsin Rashid]

The patients drafted for this [2004] study were those who had symptoms of celiac disease when on a "pure-oat" challenge. . . . This study found that 4 patients had symptoms after oat ingestion, 3 had . . . *avenin-sensitive enteropathy* (ASE). All three patients [had the] DQ2.5/DQ2 [gene]. While [this] represents only 25% of celiac patients, it accounts for all of the ASE celiacs. [Wikipedia]

Kinnikinnick Foods has taken the position that applying the "gluten-free" label to oat products would confuse consumers: Oats may be safe for some celiacs but not for all. (© Richard Levine/Alamy)

Some coeliacs respond adversely to oats. Estimates range from 0.5 to 20% of the GSE [gluten-sensitive enteropathy] population. With coeliac disease non-compliance to achieve normal intestinal morphology is a risk factor for refractory disease and cancer. [Wikipedia]

It's probably safe for most Celiacs based on a 5-year study.

For us, a 5-year study just isn't long enough when we've seen so many other things (especially chemicals & pharmaceuticals) show problems on a much longer time line (10–20+ years). Perhaps more concerning is that [according to the Canadian Celiac Association] "the studies looking at safety of oats in celiac disease have involved a small number of subjects." Let's talk in 2025 when we've had 20+ years and thousands of people studied. We'll see then if there are no issues like increased rates of cancer and other Celiac-related diseases.

It's probably safe for most Celiacs if intake is limited to around 50–70 g.

So you have your 1/2–3/4 cup oatmeal every morning. Is that enough to get you going, perhaps you need a bit more. Oh, and those oatmeal cookies are awesome so a couple at lunch or coffee are great. Maybe some haggis[1] for dinner? (Well, it's possible). Oops, you're now up to twice the recommended amount. What does that mean, long term? I don't think we really know, especially if you are getting trace amounts of other gluten proteins from cross contamination.

It's probably safe for most Celiacs if the oats are pure and uncontaminated.

A [2008] study made by a team of doctors in Spain used [four different state-of-the-art testing] techniques to evaluate 134 varieties of "pure," "uncontaminated" oats from Europe, the United States, and Canada. Results showed that just 25 of the samples were actually pure, and contained no

---

1. Haggis is the national dish of Scotland that consists of oats and sheep's internal organs cooked in a sheep's stomach.

detectable levels of contamination. The other 109 samples [of "pure" oats] all showed wheat, barley and/or rye contamination. The results also showed that contamination levels vary among oats from the same source. . . .

A Practical Approach to Oats

Now to the practical reasons.

Supply of pure, uncontaminated oats. As noted above, finding truly pure oats on a consistent basis is no small

Gluten Content in Oat Products Varies Widely

The table below shows the gluten content (based on the mean of 2 analyses) of 12 containers of rolled or steel-cut oats representing 4 different lots for each of the 3 brands purchased in Massachusetts between October 2003 and March 2004.

Product and Lot No. or Best-by Date	Gluten Content (in ppm*)
McCann's Steel-Cut Irish Oats, 28-oz container	
150134	12
150934	BLD**
270934	23
160634	725
Country Choice Old-Fashioned Organic Oats, 18-oz container	
July 13, 2004	131
December 13, 2004	210
December 17, 2004	120
March 12, 2005	BLD**
Quaker Old-Fashioned Oats, 18-oz container	
L309; January 9, 2005	338
L309; January 18, 2005	971
L110; February 12, 2005	1807
L109; March 22, 2005	364

*ppm denotes "parts per million.
**BLD denotes "below the limit of detection." The limit of gluten detection for the assay usedin this analysis was 3 ppm.

Taken from: Tricia Thompson, "Gluten Contamination of Commercial Oat Products in the United States," *New England Journal of Medicine*, May 2011.

problem. Let's assume that suppliers of pure oats have a 100% success rate and we could use them. There is still a limited, but admittedly growing supply of "pure" oats. These oats are grown by a relatively small number of farmers, often in the same area. Any problems with the crop year could cause disruptions in supply due to this small supply base. These oats are also a premium ingredient (ie: expensive) due to the labour intensive steps taken to ensure that cross contamination doesn't occur.

Oats aren't appropriate for every Celiac. Also as noted above, there is some portion of the Celiac population, perhaps as much as 20%, who can't tolerate oats. The research also shows that no one should have oats until their gut has completely healed (i.e., at least a year after diagnosis and being completely GF). Adding oats and the resulting oat cross-contamination would prevent these people from using a product. What is more concerning is the fact that these people might eat an oat-containing product, get sick and not realize why. How can you tell a customer that oat-containing products are OK for most Celiacs, but not them? In keeping with our Mission Statement of providing our customer with "a risk-free source of food products," we're just not going to "go there."

Limiting oat consumption to 50–70 g per day. How do we, as a manufacturer, manage that problem? We make our products as tasty as we possibly can. Do we add a disclaimer to our packages, "We know these are tasty, but please don't eat more than 3 of these a day because you might get sick, if not immediately, then perhaps over the long term, if you do?" I don't think so.

A little matter of the law. Lastly but definitely not least-ly, there is the little problem of the law. Currently in Canada, it is illegal to use oats in a product that is labelled gluten free. Under Section 9.9.4 Gluten-Free Foods of

FAST FACT

The most common reason for "unresponsive celiac disease," where patients show no improvement on a gluten-free diet, is the presence of small amounts of gluten still in the diet.

the Food Labelling & Advertising Act: "A food is not permitted to be labelled, packaged, sold or advertised in a manner likely to create an impression that it is 'gluten-free' unless it does not contain wheat, including spelt and kamut, or oats, barley, rye, triticale or any part thereof."

That's pretty much the show stopper right there. Even if we had no misgivings about using oats and we had solved all the practical issues, we couldn't do it the way the law is currently written. Given the speed of governments on issues like this, we can probably look forward to a change in, oh, 2025. Which might be a good thing. We might finally know by then whether oats are safe. It's important to note that these are concerns based on our reading of the literature and many will say that they are unfounded and that's fine. Am I saying oats aren't safe for Celiacs? No. I'm saying that I'm not convinced there is enough long term evidence to say one way or the other. We aren't going to make any kind of change regarding oats until these questions of long term safety are answered to our satisfaction. Oh, and the law changes.

CHAPTER 3

Personal Narratives

A Mother Witnesses Her Daughter Suffering from Undiagnosed Celiac Disease

Susan Blumenfeld

In the following personal story, Susan Blumenfeld describes the agonizing and helpless feeling of watching the health of Julie, her toddler daughter, decline precipitously. Julie vomited constantly, was pale and thin, and had a distended belly. With Blumenfeld's prodding, Julie's pediatrician ordered myriad tests to look for various medical disorders. Celiac disease, however, was not considered. It was not until a pediatric gastroenterologist guessed that Julie had celiac disease, and she was started on a gluten-free diet, that Blumenfeld finally saw her daughter regain her health.

The week of my 35th birthday, my daughter Julie lay dying on a hospital gurney, waiting to receive general anesthesia. Not even two years old, Julie was very familiar with hospitals and tests. She was about to have an MRI to find out why she had lost so much weight, stopped walking, continued to vomit and pass

Photo on facing page. Many restaurants are now offering gluten-free meals on their menus. (© AP Images/ Gregory Bull)

SOURCE: Susan Blumenfeld, "Susan's Story: A Mother's Struggle to Find the True Cause of Her Daughter's Illness," UCHospitals.edu, 2011.

stools that looked like undigested food. It was hard to believe that only six months ago she was a happy and healthy baby, with pudgy cheeks and lots of energy. Now, she could barely hold her head up, and inside I was screaming, because there was nothing I could do to make it stop.

And her doctors couldn't figure out what was wrong with her.

My Baby's Declining Health

When Julie was 18 months old, my husband Levi and I began to notice changes in her appearance, especially when it was bath time. Her belly had become big and round, and her shoulder blades became very prominent. Her rear end had all but disappeared.

Around the same time, Julie began vomiting often— often enough that I would carry a change of her clothes, plenty of towels and wipes to clean her up afterwards, in the car, in the park, in a restaurant, in the grocery store. Julie became miserably unhappy and cried a lot, only wanting to be held.

Initially, when we saw our pediatrician, she said Julie looked fine, probably had lactose intolerance and felt that she was going through the "terrible twos" a little early. She recommended a book. My gut instinct told me that she was wrong, and that Julie was very ill. She could no longer attend preschool.

The vomiting continued, and my daughter's health declined. My friends and family would ask, "What's wrong with Julie?" I became frantic. By now, my daughter's diapers were full of stool that looked like undigested food and when I changed them the smell was terrible— not normal. It appeared to me that she wasn't getting her basic nutritional needs met—and I struggled to find something she could eat that would help her.

She continued to vomit, and each time, I called the pediatrician's office insisting that something was really wrong. Our pediatrician swung into action and began to order tests. She ordered blood tests, a kidney scan, a barium swallow and dozens more tests. It got to the point where Julie and I would go to the hospital two or three times a week for blood work, all while she continued to decline. She was tested for cystic fibrosis, where a hot copper coil was placed on her arm—and her arm was wrapped in plastic for a "sweat test." They looked for brain tumors, GI [gastrointestinal] blockages and kidney disease.

She looked so sickly, like a starving child in a third world country. I've thrown away the worst pictures of her at this time because they are too difficult for me to look at.

She was diagnosed with cytomegalovirus and hepatitis, yet did not improve. My husband and I were elated to reach a diagnosis, then devastated when she continued to worsen. Levi is a medical doctor, and researched Julie's condition thoroughly, shortly after she became ill. When we asked Julie's doctors if they had considered celiac disease, they dismissed our suggestion with little more than a wave of the hand.

Five days after an MRI, a noted pediatric gastroenterologist came to see Julie. He took one look at her and told us she had celiac disease. The next day—my 35th birthday—she had an endoscopic biopsy and received the diagnosis. She's been on the gluten-free diet (the only treatment for celiac disease) ever since, and we have our daughter back.

Celiac disease is a common, inherited gastrointestinal autoimmune disorder that affects 1.4 million Americans—yet most physicians receive 20 minutes of instruction on it in medical school. Every day that a person with celiac disease goes undiagnosed, their risk of developing autoimmune disorders, neurological disorders, osteoporosis, infertility, and even cancer, increases

FAST FACT

According to the Children's Digestive Health and Nutrition Foundation, approximately one in three hundred to one in eighty children between the ages of two-and-a-half and fifteen years old have celiac disease.

greatly. Yet there are one million cases of celiac disease that go undiagnosed in this country.

That's why I've helped create the University of Chicago Celiac Disease Center, an organization with a mission to improve the lives of celiac patients and to raise diagnosis rates by advancing research on celiac disease and increasing awareness among medical professionals and the public.

So that children don't have to suffer. So that doctors think of celiac disease first, and not last.

A Television Personality Struggles for Years with Undiagnosed Celiac Disease

Elisabeth Hasselbeck

According to Elisabeth Hasselbeck in the following viewpoint, pasta and breads filled with gluten were a big part of her childhood. By the time she was in college, the symptoms of celiac disease had begun to show up. Hasselbeck describes years of painful and debilitating intestinal problems and numerous doctors misdiagnosing her with intestinal infections, irritable bowel syndrome, and even stress. Going to the Australian Outback as a participant on the reality TV show *Survivor* led Hasselbeck to a self-diagnosis, which was later confirmed, of celiac disease.

Hasselbeck is a cohost of the TV show *The View* and author of the book *The G-Free Diet: A Gluten Survival Guide*.

I learned about gluten the hard way. I wrote this book so you don't have to. Most people with celiac disease, like me, have a story to tell. My hope is that in reading mine, and the pages that follow, you will be able to

SOURCE: Elisabeth Hasselbeck, "Elisabeth Hasselback Explains Her Gluten-Free Lifestyle," ABC News, May 5, 2009. www.abcnews .go.com. Copyright © 2009 by ABCNews.com. All rights reserved. Reproduced by permission.

begin your journey to a better body and a better self—without all the heartache (and bellyache!) that I endured for far too long.

Bread and Pasta All the Time

I grew up in an Italian-American neighborhood in Providence, Rhode Island. There wasn't a single holiday that did not feature "Mama's" (my grandmother's) famous baked penne along with a thirty-inch loaf of fresh Italian bread. After dessert, my whole family would even sit around dunking any remaining bread into our coffee. My cousins and I would fight over who got the "end" of each loaf. I remember watching Mama slice into the loaf, waiting to see if it was my "day" or not. The smell of more toasted Italian bread and butter would wake me up the next morning.

In my childhood home, it was all bread, all the time—and that was just the way we liked it.

While some things haven't changed in my family—we still have baked penne at every holiday dinner—other things certainly have. Since 2002, for example, my mom has made two baked penne: one for everyone else, and one just for me, a gluten-free version that hurts neither my stomach nor Mama's feelings when she looks over and sees a plate devoid of our traditional family fare.

"What do you mean you 'can't have the penne'?" Mama would question me after we sat down at her table. Over and over, I would try to explain to my grandmother, whom I love with my whole heart, and hated to upset at all, that "I am allergic to the pasta."

"Since when?" she would immediately shoot back.

The answer to that was a bit more complicated.

Difficulties Begin

The trouble began in early 1997, during the spring of my sophomore year of college. I went on two big trips that spring. The first, over winter break, was a three-week-long immersion/teaching trip to the village of Red Bank and the city of Dangriga in Belize [Central America]. The second, a spring training trip, was within the United States, with my Boston College softball team.

I had been feeling a little under the weather since Belize, and shortly after I returned from the softball trip, I was diagnosed with a severe bacterial intestinal infection—residue, the doctor said, from my trip to Central America. I landed in the school infirmary for nearly a week, with an immensely distended belly and a 103- to 104-degree fever. My memories of that week are hazy at best: I can recall little more than opening my eyes to see my mom standing over the bed. And Tim, my college sweetheart and now husband, looking more than concerned.

Once the initial infection had subsided, I was incredibly relieved, thinking I was finally in the clear. As an athlete, I couldn't bear the thought of being "off my game" for more than a day or two. Little did I suspect that my game was going to be significantly "off" for quite some time....

After leaving the infirmary, I was eager to get my body back on track again, but my digestive system was seemingly shot. My efforts to regain some of the muscle mass I had lost during my convalescence went nowhere. And though I felt ravenously hungry all the time, the only dining hall option that looked even remotely appetizing to me was soft-serve vanilla frozen yogurt with Rice Krispies mixed in. Food just didn't appeal to me like it had before.

Regardless, I continued to eat, though nothing satisfied my hunger—and everything seemed to throw my stomach into a frenzy. Each meal left me bloated and gassy, with sharp, explosive pains in my abdomen. No matter what I ate, I would soon be doubled over with cramps, awful indigestion, diarrhea—or all of the above simultaneously. I soon became all too familiar with the location of any and all bathrooms. Half an hour later, I would be too lethargic to move.

What on earth was happening to me? I had always been filled with energy before, and now I wanted to crawl back into bed five times a day. I was always in pain, always uncomfortable—especially around mealtimes.

Food Became My Enemy

Food, for the first time to this pasta-loving girl, had become the enemy. I was at war with my own body, and it soon became obvious that I was losing each and every battle.

Early on, I (and everyone around me) attributed my difficulties to stress, combined with a lingering infection in my gut. But as time went on and I made my first career move out of school—working as a footwear designer for PUMA—my health only worsened. I was barely able to get through the day without being sideswiped by extreme pain and overwhelming fatigue. I would retreat to the bathroom every ten minutes or so, locking myself in a stall and pressing on my belly in an effort to get control of the spastic bouts in my intestinal region. To keep my colleagues from suspecting that I was under the weather all the time, I would strategically walk a different way to the ladies' room each time, to avoid passing the same person twice in a row.

My commute to and from the office was even more distressing. I was constantly pulling over to the side of the road: Intense pain in my lower abdomen made it nearly impossible for me to sit up straight and focus on driving. The pain typically worsened throughout the day. I would get home from work and try different strategies to "move" whatever was causing the pain. After numerous trips to the bathroom, I could only get relief by lying on my side in bed.

"Stress" was just not cutting it as the explanation for my pain. I was twenty-three and supposedly healthy, but I wasn't. Was I simply doomed to spend the rest of my life in digestive agony? Such a bleak conclusion was not acceptable. My gut instinct (pun intended) told me there was more to learn.

Searching for Answers

I began to search for answers in earnest, but all my doctors' appointments stuck to the same script. An identical examination, followed by an identical diagnosis:

"IBS."

"Irritable bowel syndrome."

"IBS . . . it's becoming quite common."

Over and over again, that's what I was told. But the only accurate part of the term "IBS," in my opinion, was the "BS." Possibly, this diagnosis was "quite common"—because the doctors were quite commonly missing the cause. No mention of a food allergy ever came up, despite my repeated indications that I felt the worst immediately after eating. The doctors refused to see the connection between what I was eating and how I was feeling.

After more fruitless examinations than I care to remember, I was completely fed up. I was also in unbelievable pain around the clock. At that point, I was willing to try absolutely anything to get answers. After undergoing a "recommended" sigmoidoscopy—a minimally invasive intestinal procedure that yielded no clear diagnosis—I began to feel even worse. None of the medication I was prescribed for my stomach seemed to help, and I was tired of relying on doctors for solutions that never seemed to come. One doctor actually put me on an antianxiety pill. The reason? One of the medication's side effects was that it numbed the stomach lining. The doctor had completely missed the mark.

Researching It for Myself

That day set me, fuming, on a more determined search. There had to be a more direct means of treating whatever was going on with me. I refused to spend the rest of my life bouncing from doctor to doctor—or taking serious

Television personality Elisabeth Hasselbeck, author of this viewpoint, has written a cookbook, *The G-Free Diet: A Gluten-Free Survival Guide*. (© Gilbert Carrasquillo/ FilmMagic/Getty Images)

prescription drugs hoping for their side effects to kick in. If my own physicians were not helping me, I was going to get to the bottom of this mystery on my own.

From that day forward, I dove into research. I met with a holistic doctor in a neighboring state, who put me on a dairy-free, lactose-free, yeast-free program. Under his care, I went on a whole regimen of supplements and vitamins, and I lived off these special bars, which I was allowed to eat three times a day. I ate apricot seeds every day, as he told me they would help. The seeds were the most vile-tasting things I had ever tasted, but I kept on eating them in the hopes of feeling better. Even though they seemed to burn my tongue, I was willing to give them a shot. To my dismay, not even these extreme measures brought about any significant changes in my condition. Still, I resolved to do whatever it took. If that guy had told me to stand on my head for ten minutes every hour, I would gladly have done it for eleven.

The Adventure That Saved My Life

As we were about to begin the phase of removing wheat from my diet, I applied to become a contestant on the reality show *Survivor: The Australian Outback*. Throughout the selection process, I hid my symptoms from the producers, saying nothing about the stomach pain that I was experiencing. As I went through extensive physical exams, I was amazed that no one could tell that the inside of my body was a complete disaster. I held back tears during one exam, which entailed the doctor pressing on my stomach. I held my breath as the doctor told me I was "good to go" . . . secretly counting the seconds until I could race to the bathroom.

Early the next morning, miraculously enough, I was picked as a contestant on *Survivor*, and so off I went, pain and all, into the Outback.

My Australian adventure was nothing short of life-altering. It was an incredibly rich, rewarding time—physically, mentally, and spiritually. Not surprisingly, it was the most physically grueling experience of my life. I was also given the most wonderful opportunity to investigate how my body works. Though exhausted on every level, I felt awakened. I learned how to live off the earth, to respect its boundaries, to work and bond with strangers, and to get by without any creature comforts. I also learned what mattered to me most, and what I relied on in extreme circumstances. One other remarkable thing happened to me Down Under, too: For the first time in about three years, I felt no pain in my stomach.

I remember thinking on multiple occasions, "Even though I haven't showered in thirty-nine days, I feel clean and pure." I was fairly certain that this sensation had nothing to do with my skin or hair or scent, and everything to do with my internal system. I was completely detoxified—without pain, without cramping or bloating, without any intestinal symptoms at all. I felt like I had before I had checked into the college infirmary so long ago. That person seemed to be nearly forgotten.

Shockingly, it took starving in the Outback of Australia to feel like myself again. I remember joking that "I must be allergic to the United States." That was not the case.

I had lost about twenty pounds, but though my belly was empty, I left Australia full of answers. I left knowing that without God, I had nothing; that my family was the most incredible source of support; that I never again wanted to be away from Tim. I left knowing that for the past three years, my body had been fighting something that I was eating at home, and that if I didn't take it upon myself to figure out what that food was, no one else would do it for me. Once I was back home, the scope of my quest narrowed.

On the Trail of the Culprit

Energized with the sense that I was on the trail of the culprit at last, and with a clean slate, I decided to reintroduce one item at a time back into my diet. But after thirty-nine days in near-starvation mode, I was absolutely ravenous, and I wasn't about to give up my favorite foods without a fight. Soon, despite my best intentions, I had returned to my pre-Australia diet, and the consequences were dire. After the relief of having had my gut repaired, now I was suddenly feeling worse than ever, spending day after day in my room, unable to get out of bed, except to race to the bathroom.

They say that every cloud has a silver lining, and this horrible time finally clued me in to the cause of my long illness. I noticed that the moment I ate a starchy food, all the symptoms returned, and with even more fury than before. I went on the Internet to research what this reaction might mean, and soon after thought I had discovered the cause: Wheat! Out it went from my diet.

There were some days when I didn't feel so bad. Still, every so often, I would get tripped up after eating sushi or teriyaki chicken, and I couldn't put my finger on what was making me sick. After more and more online research, I stumbled upon some information about gluten intolerance and celiac disease. In 2002, five years since the onset of my symptoms, I diagnosed myself with celiac disease, an autoimmune condition triggered by gluten, the protein found in everything from pasta to bread to cookies. The only known treatment for celiac disease—which can cause acute damage to the small intestine and the digestive system as a whole—is a lifelong gluten-free diet.

FAST FACT

Experts estimate that 36 percent of individuals diagnosed with celiac disease were initially given a diagnosis of irritable bowel syndrome.

Doctors in Denial

Since celiac disease seemed to cover each of the symptoms that had been plaguing me for so many years, I set about eliminating all wheat, then barley, oats, and rye—the main gluten-containing foods—from my diet. In the beginning, the road was rocky: There was so much I still had to learn about gluten, and finding desirable alternatives was not as easy as it is today. I also found myself repeatedly rebelling against my self-diagnosis, and bingeing on gluten-containing foods just to prove that I could have them if I wanted to. Despite these repeated slipups, I nevertheless persevered . . . And my body would soon thank me.

Even after this breakthrough, doctors resisted my self-diagnosis. Though I was convinced that I had celiac disease—and armed with plenty of specific examples to back up my claim—I still could not find a physician who would run the necessary diagnostic tests on me. Dismissing the theory that my diet could cure me, doctor after doctor kept on prescribing medications that did little more than mask my symptoms, if even that.

I began to wonder why so many doctors ignored my theory—and why I had to spend months learning about celiac disease on my own. There had to be a reason why such a common disease, which affects an estimated 1 out of every 100 to 200 people worldwide, was not on medical radar at all. The more I thought about it, the more I came to believe that there was no money in researching gluten intolerance, because there was no medication to treat it. No noise, no advertisement, no call to diagnose. Was this the result of some conspiracy? Neglect? Straight-up ignorance? Whatever the explanation, I had to struggle for eight long years before I found a physician who was willing to listen, willing to run proper tests, and willing to join me on the voyage that I'd been on since 1997.

Finally, a Diagnosis

Ironically, I had to travel all the way to Australia to gain real insights into what was hurting me in the United States, and when I moved to New York City, it was an Australian, Dr. Peter Green, the director of the Celiac Disease Center at Columbia University, who confirmed what I'd suspected for years. The moment he told me I had a disease—celiac disease—I enthusiastically thanked him. This reaction might seem a little bit odd, but I had been searching for a clear-cut diagnosis for almost a decade by then! I had consulted innumerable experts in the hopes of finding out what was wrong with me. For all those years I had waited in vain for an explanation that made sense. Dr. Green was the first doctor to look for the cause, not simply treat the symptoms. My gratitude to him is beyond measure.

Once Dr. Green confirmed that I had celiac disease, I became even more committed to what I called the G-free lifestyle. With Dr. Green's help, I deepened my knowledge of where gluten is found, and how I could most effectively avoid it. With the encouragement of my loved ones, I became more adept at shopping for and preparing delicious G-free alternatives to what had once been my favorite foods.

In no time at all, I found that living G-free wasn't so bad at all! In fact, I've never felt better in my life. I cannot imagine ever returning to eating gluten—even if I didn't have celiac disease. The G-free diet gives me the stamina and strength I need to manage my increasingly hectic life.

It turns out I have a lot of company! Apparently, I am not alone in benefiting from the G-free diet: According to the University of Chicago, 1 out of every 133 otherwise healthy adults in the United States has celiac disease—that's nearly 3 million of us.

Suffering from a Mysterious Complication of Celiac Disease

Jonathan Papernick

In the following personal story, Jonathan Papernick talks about being stricken with a mysterious illness after recovering from celiac disease. According to Papernick, the intestinal damage caused by celiac disease made him vulnerable to a yeast infection, the symptoms of which made him feel like he was dying. Papernick says that he saw several doctors before one finally pinpointed the cause of his sickness. He thinks there are probably many other celiac patients who suffer needlessly because doctors are unfamiliar with the complications of celiac disease.

Papernick is a fiction writer and has taught fiction writing at various universities, including Brandeis University and Emerson College. There Is No Other, a collection of his stories, was published in 2010.

The problems began not long after I moved in with my future wife. I was losing weight at an alarming rate, drifting for hours after meals in a confused fog. My acid reflux was so bad I felt like I had a golf ball lodged in my throat. I suffered from otherworldly constipation and had no sex drive. My tongue swelled like a wet sponge. It seemed everything I ate contributed to my misery.

These symptoms weren't the ones familiar to me from my mid-20s, when I'd learned I had celiac disease. People with celiac can't tolerate gluten, a protein in wheat found in many foods and everyday products. When I ate gluten, my sides ached and my small intestines felt as if they had been rubbed raw by sandpaper; I felt tremors throughout my body and deep, deep exhaustion. My mother lived with celiac disease for most of her life, and after overcoming years of willful ignorance of my mother's condition, my health finally improved when I began avoiding wheat and other gluten-containing grains.

Even Gluten-Free Foods Made Me Sick

Now even gluten-free foods caused my throat to tickle and my head to throb, and I had no idea why. I had painful canker sores all the time. I couldn't understand how I could have solved one mystery by removing gluten from my diet, only to be baffled by another, more frightening, condition.

My future wife was afraid I was dying and wondered seriously whether I was somehow allergic to her. By the time we were married a year later, several allergists had told me that I had no allergies at all. Gastrointestinal doctors blamed my mysterious affliction on stress. An acupuncturist said my *chi* was out of whack. I was tested for parasites and came up clean. More than a few friends and family members suggested indelicately that my problems were all in my head, or worse still, that I was simply seeking attention. I couldn't even look at the skeleton resembling myself in the mirror anymore.

Illness can do strange things to an ordinarily rational mind, and I was desperate to find a solution. A friend told me about a new-age treatment that claimed to resolve undiagnosed health problems. After shelling out several hundred dollars for a consultation, I was informed that my problems were caused by "energy blockages," disruptions in the normal flow of energy through my body's electrical circuits. The practitioner said she could permanently cure me simply by treating my pressure points while I held in my hand a vial of charged water containing the same properties as the allergen. Apparently, a minimum of 30 to 40 treatments would be necessary to help me gain back chicken, potatoes, rice, beans and other staples that I had relied on my entire life. For more than six months I paid good money for treatments that did nothing to help me, the practitioner always promising that next time I was due for a breakthrough that would allow me to once again eat my favorite foods. I should have been more skeptical of this miracle cure. But with more and more foods finding their way onto my blacklist, I could not afford cynicism. I needed a miracle and nothing less.

My wife had had enough of my indulgence in expensive, unproven "voodoo" medicine, and she put out a frantic call to her friends and colleagues asking for help. A friend passed along the name of a doctor known to have success with people thought of as incurable—the last resort for many seemingly hopeless cases.

Celiacs Vulnerable to Yeasts and Molds

Within minutes of meeting the doctor and explaining my symptoms, he was certain that he had pinpointed the source of all my problems. Yeast. He took a blood test just to be sure, and as predicted, my yeast levels were off the charts. He explained how *Candida albicans,* an aggressive sugar-eating yeast that had been colonizing my intestines, is a common concern for celiacs, whose tiny, hair-like villi in their intestines have been flattened and damaged by gluten.

Under normal circumstances, the majority of the human population lives with *Candida albicans* in their digestive systems without any problems. But I listened with horror as he explained how the roots of the *Candida* were starting to break through the walls of my intestinal tract, causing a leaky gut through which microscopic bits of food were entering my bloodstream.

I was ordered to cut out all sugar, alcohol, fruit, starch, peanuts and mushrooms and told to eat protein and vegetables with low sugar content. I was allowed kale and collard greens, but carrots and red peppers were off the list. I was taking no less than 12 different supplements, including probiotics and digestive enzymes, to heal my system. My compromised digestive system couldn't even handle ordinary calcium supplements, and my wife and I sat at our coffee table filling gelatin capsules with white calcium powder. (You can imagine what it looked like to an unknowing visitor [that they were measuring out cocaine].)

The doctor prescribed an antifungal that would work slowly to kill off the unwelcome aggressor. Every time I

Candida albicans is a yeast that inhabits the mouth, throat, urinary tract, and intestines of humans. If unchecked, *Candida* roots break through the walls of the intestines, causing microscopic bits of undigested food to enter the bloodstream. (© Stem Jems/Photo Researchers, Inc.)

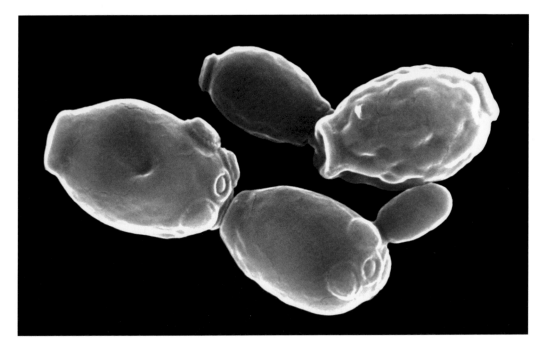

took the medication, even at the lowest possible dose, I felt like I'd been struck down by the flu as the invading yeasts died off—evidence of how serious my problem was. It would take a long time to reverse the damage that the *Candida* had done, but I was finally on the right track.

When I didn't improve as quickly as my doctor expected, he sent a mold remediation specialist out to our apartment to check out our living situation. There was black mold in our closets and on our walls, and the air shaft that was supposed to provide fresh air to three of our rooms was full of pigeon feces and filth. I was shocked to learn that our New York City apartment was slowly killing me.

My doctor explained that others could live perfectly normal lives with this mold, but in my case, with a compromised immune system, the toxic mold was simply piling on a heavily taxed system and adding fuel to the *Candida*—the literal last straw. We were ordered to clean our walls with hydrogen peroxide and to purchase an industrial-strength air filter with an infrared beam to get rid of the mold. The hydrogen peroxide had little effect, as the tenacious mold seemed to reappear within days.

I slowly reintroduced foods back into my diet, starting with a simple forkful at a time. However, with every slice of potato, mouthful of rice, nibble of chicken, I felt my head throb, my throat tickle. My doctor suggested that we move, and before long, a job opened up in Boston. I packed up and left town—four months ahead of my wife, who still needed to wrap up things with her job.

FAST FACT

According to a study published in 2010, about 34 percent of celiac sufferers' intestines have still not healed five years after going gluten-free.

Unnecessary Suffering

Within weeks of living in New England, I started to improve, slowly, ever so slowly, and I found the courage to reintroduce foods back into my diet. It took years, not months, as I followed the doctor's strict diet, which included egg whites and spinach and tuna for breakfast. Eventually, gradually, thankfully I got better.

I have since gained the weight back (and then some) and have started a family. With the increased availability of allergen-free medicines and supplements, and my own hard-learned lessons, I am now able to enjoy life all over again. But I can't help but wonder how many people with celiac disease have suffered unnecessarily because so many doctors are not prepared to deal effectively with the condition.

GLOSSARY

amino acid	Biological molecules that assemble together to produce proteins.
antibody	A specialized protein produced by the immune system to recognize and attack foreign cells or substances, such as bacteria and viruses. The foreign substances recognized by antibodies are called antigens. Antibodies are also known as immunoglobulins.
antiendomysial antibodies (EMA)	Autoantibodies that recognize endomysial tissue. People with celiac disease generally have high levels of these autoantibodies.
antigen	Cells or substances, or components of cells or substances, that are recognized by antibodies and attacked by the immune system.
anti-tissue transglutaminase antibodies (tTGA)	Autoantibodies that recognizes the enzyme tissue transglutaminase. High levels of these autoantibodies are strongly linked to celiac disease.
autoantibody	An antibody that perceives the body's own cells or tissues as invaders and attacks them.
autoimmune disease	A disease in which the immune system goes awry and mistakenly attacks the body's own cells and tissues.
biopsy	A medical test in which cells or tissues are removed from the body and examined to determine whether a disease is present.
bowel	Another name for the intestine. The small bowel and the large bowel are the small intestine and large intestine, respectively.
celiac	A term derived from the Latin word *coeliacus* (itself derived from the Greek *koiliakos*), meaning "of or relating to the abdomen or abdominal cavity."

celiac (or coeliac) disease	A disorder resulting from an immune reaction to gluten, a protein found in wheat and related grains and present in many foods.
celiac sprue	Another name for celiac disease.
cereal grains	The edible seeds of plants from the grass family such as barley, oats, rice, rye, wheat. Also called merely "cereals."
chronic disease	A disease that persists for a long time. According to the US National Center for Health Statistics, chronic diseases are those that last longer than three months. Celiac disease is a chronic disease.
colon	The large intestine.
dermatitis herpetiformis	A chronic and extremely itchy rash of bumps and blisters that is associated with celiac disease.
diarrhea	Unusually frequent and/or unusually loose bowel movements.
endomysial	Relating to the endomysium.
endomysium	The layer of connective tissue that ensheaths muscle fibers.
enteropathy	Disease of the intestine.
enzyme	A type of protein that catalyzes, or helps initiate or complete, a chemical reaction. There are thousands of enzymes in the human body that serve crucial functions in practically every cellular process that occurs. Enzymes are essential for the function of any biological system.
epithelium	A term used to describe body tissues (including the gastrointestinal tract lining) that help protect organs or surfaces that have direct contact with anything from the outside world.
gastroenterology	The medical specialty devoted to the study, diagnosis, and treatment of disorders of the digestive system.
gastrointestinal	A term referring collectively to the stomach and small and large intestines.

Gee-Herter disease	The name given to celiac disease early in the twentieth century before its cause was discovered. It refers to physicians Samuel Gee and Christian Herter.
gliadin	A prolamin, or plant storage protein, that is present in wheat and certain other cereals and is a component of gluten.
gluten	A protein composite found in wheat and certain other cereal grains. The term *gluten* is derived from the Latin word for "glue," and gives elasticity to dough, helping it to rise and to keep its shape.
gluten enteropathy	Another name for celiac disease.
gluten sensitivity	A disorder caused by gluten that is similar to but distinct from celiac disease.
glycoprotein	A protein with a carbohydrate (sugar) component.
immunoglobulin	A protein that functions as an antibody.
latent celiac disease	Refers to people who test positive for celiac disease antibodies but who have no intestinal damage or symptoms. These people can develop symptoms of celiac disease later in life.
malabsorption	A difficulty digesting or absorbing nutrients from food.
mucosal	Refers to tissues that secrete mucus, such as the linings of external cavities, including the nose, and of internal organs, such as the intestines.
nontropical sprue	Another name for celiac disease.
prolamines	A group of plant storage proteins that have a high content of the amino acid proline.
proteines	Large biological molecules composed of amino acids that have myriad important functions in the body.

serological test   Any of several laboratory procedures carried out on a sample of blood serum, the clear liquid that separates from the blood when it is allowed to clot. The purpose of such a test is to detect serum antibodies or antibody-like substances that appear specifically in association with certain diseases.

silent celiac disease   Refers to people who test positive for celiac disease antibodies and have a loss of villi in the small intestine but have no symptoms or signs of celiac disease, even on a diet that contains gluten. These people can develop signs or symptoms of celiac disease later in life.

sprue   Another name for celiac disease.

tissue transglutaminase   Any one of a group of important enzymes that are involved in the conversion of the amino acid glutamine into the amino acid glutamate.

villi   Hairlike projections that cover the lining of the small intestine and help absorb nutrients.

villous atrophy   The damage of the intestinal villi.

CHRONOLOGY

100 Greek physician Aretaeus the Cappadocian describes a disease he calls *koiliakos* ("abdominal"). Aretaeus states, "If the stomach be irretentive of food and if it pass through undigested and crude, and nothing ascends into the body, we call such persons coeliacs."

1669 Dutch physician Vincent Ketelaer publishes a book that contains an account of a diarrheal illness in which he notes feces so voluminous that, "several basins or pots scarcely hold these accumulations."

1888 British physician Samuel Gee publishes his classic paper "On the Coeliac Affection" and suggests that "if the patient can be cured at all, it must be by means of diet."

1889 British physician R.A. Gibbons publishes "The Celiac Affection in Children" in the *Edinburgh Medical Journal*.

1908 American physician Christian Herter discovers that celiac disease can cause stunted growth.

1921 British physician John Howland devises a three-stage diet for celiac patients known as the milk/protein diet.

1924 American pediatrician Sidney Haas describes a treatment of celiac disease known as the banana diet.

1932 Danish physician Thorwald Thaysen provides a clinical explanation of celiac disease in adults.

1936   Dutch pediatrician Willem-Karel Dicke isolates cereal grains as a factor in aggravating the symptoms of celiac disease, especially in children, and begins treating children with a gluten-free diet.

1941   Dicke publishes a report about a wheat-free diet as a treatment for Gee-Herter disease, later known as celiac disease.

1952   Sydney Haas and his son Merrill publish *The Management of Celiac Disease.*

1954   British physician J.W. Paulley experiments with surgical biopsy material and discovers the intestinal lesions caused by celiac disease.

1956   British physician Margot Shiner invents a tiny biopsy tube to confirm the presence of celiac disease in the small intestines.

1968   A relationship between celiac disease and dermatitis herpetiformis, an itchy skin rash, is established by British dermatologists Sam Shuster and Janet Marks.

1970   Antibodies recognizing the gluten constituent glycoprotein gliadin are discovered.

1980s   Antibodies recognizing endomysial tissue (the membrane surrounding smooth muscles) are discovered and are used to screen for celiac disease.

1997   German researcher Walburga Dieterich identifies the autoantibody for celiac disease (which recognizes the enzyme transglutaminase), leading to a highly specific screening test for celiac disease.

2004   The US Congress passes the Food Allergen Labeling and Consumer Protection Act.

2007   The US Food and Drug Administration (FDA) proposes issuing regulations regarding the use of the term "gluten-free" on food labels.

2011   The FDA announces that it is reopening the public comment period on the gluten-free labeling proposal it issued in 2007.

ORGANIZATIONS TO CONTACT

The editors have compiled the following list of organizations concerned with the issues debated in this book. The descriptions are derived from materials provided by the organizations. All have publications or information available for interested readers. The list was compiled on the date of publication of the present volume; the information provided here may change. Be aware that many organizations take several weeks or longer to respond to inquiries, so allow as much time as possible.

American Celiac Disease Alliance (ACDA)
2504 Duxbury Pl.
Alexandria, VA 22308
(703) 622-3331
e-mail: info@american celiac.org
website: www.american celiac.org

The ACDA is a nonprofit organization that was originally formed to improve American food-labeling laws. Since then, the mission of the organization has expanded. The alliance works to advance education about and research into celiac disease and to advocate on behalf of the entire celiac community—patients, physicians, researchers, food manufacturers, and other service providers. The ACDA provides guidance to the US government and food manufacturers on issues relating to celiac disease. The group's website provides resources about living with celiac disease for families, health professionals, and others.

American Dietetic Association (ADA)
120 S. Riverside Plaza
Ste. 2000, Chicago, IL 60606-6995
(800) 877-1600
e-mail: hotline@eat right.org
website: www.eatright .org

The ADA is an organization of dietary and nutrition professionals who are committed to improving the nation's health and advancing the profession of dietetics through research, education, and advocacy. The ADA accomplishes its mission by providing reliable and evidence-based nutrition information to the public, by acting as the accrediting agency for graduate and undergraduate nutritional education curricula, credentialing dietetics professionals, and by advocating for public policy issues affecting consumers and the practice of dietetics, including Medicare coverage of medical nutrition therapy; licensure of registered dietitians; child nutrition; obesity; food safety; the Dietary Guidelines for Americans; and other health and nutrition priorities. The ADA publishes a monthly peer-reviewed periodical, the *Journal of the American Dietetic Association*.

Celiac Disease Foundation (CDF)
13251 Ventura Blvd., #1
Studio City, CA 91604
(818) 990-2354
fax: (818) 990-2379
e-mail: cdf@celiac.org
website: www.celiac.org

The mission of the CDF is to educate, inform, and raise the public's awareness about celiac disease. The foundation also seeks to advocate for celiac disease sufferers and provide support services to both the lay as well as the professional health communities. CDF sponsors many activities to achieve its mission, including a gluten-free summer camp for kids, Team Gluten-Free races around the country, expos, fairs, and celiac disease–screening events. The CDF website provides various celiac disease resources, including research reports and articles from the peer-reviewed journal *Practical Gastroenterology*.

Celiac Sprue Association (CSA)
PO Box 31700,
Omaha, NE 68131-0700
(877) 272-4272
e-mail: www.csaceliacs
.info/contact_us.jsp
website: www.csaceliacs
.info

The CSA pursues a mission that dedicates its efforts to helping individuals with celiac disease and gluten sensitivities through research, education, and support. The group works locally, regionally, and nationally to increase awareness, improve diagnosis and treatment, and help celiacs and gluten-sensitive individuals to be happy living gluten-free. The CSA quarterly newsletter provides updates on research, legislative concerns, gluten-free product news, and labeling, among other things.

Gluten Intolerance Group of North America (GIG)
31214 124th Ave. SE
Auburn, WA 98092
(253) 833-6655
fax: (253) 833-6675
e-mail: info@gluten.net
website: www.gluten.net

The GIG is a nonprofit organization that works to provide support to persons with gluten intolerances, including celiac disease, dermatitis herpetiformis, and other gluten sensitivities. GIG programs include the Gluten-Free Certification Organization, which certifies gluten-free foods, and the Gluten-Free Restaurant Awareness Program, which informs the public about restaurants offering gluten-free menu items. The organization publishes a magazine for kids called the *Celiac Kids Magazine*. The organization's website includes a blog.

National Foundation for Celiac Awareness (NFCA)
224 S. Maple St.
Ambler, PA 19002-0544
(215) 325-1306
e-mail: info@celiac central.org
website: www.celiac central.org

The mission of the NFCA is to raise awareness and funding for celiac disease that will facilitate research, diagnosis, screening, and education to improve the quality of life of children and adults affected by this autoimmune disease. The foundation's website provides information for celiac disease patients, the parents of children with the disease, those who think they may have celiac disease, and anyone wanting to learn about the disease and how to live with it. NFCA's monthly newsletter covers a variety of topics, including celiac disease news, lifestyle and wellness information, gluten-free product reviews, and recipes, as well as NFCA programming and event updates.

National Institute of Diabetes and Digestive and Kidney Diseases (NIDDK)
31 Center Dr., Bldg. 31 Rm. 9A06, MSC 2560
Bethesda, MD 20892-2560
(301) 496-3583
e-mail: nddic@info.nid dk.nih.gov
website: www.digestive .niddk.nih.gov

The NIDDK is one of the twenty-seven institutes and centers that compose the National Institutes of Health. The institute conducts and supports basic and clinical research on diseases such as diabetes, obesity, inborn errors of metabolism, endocrine disorders, mineral metabolism, digestive and liver diseases, urology and renal disease, and hematology. The institute provides comprehensive and current information about celiac and other digestive diseases at the National Digestive Diseases Information Clearinghouse, available at its website. The Celiac Disease Awareness Campaign sponsored by the NIDDK also provides comprehensive information about celiac disease.

North American Society for Pediatric Gastroenterology, Hepatology and Nutrition (NASPGHAN)
PO Box 6, Flourtown PA 19031
(215) 233-0808
fax: (215) 233-3918
e-mail: naspghan@ naspghan.org
website: www.naspghan .org

The mission of the NASPGHAN is to advance understanding of normal development, physiology, and pathophysiology of diseases of the gastrointestinal tract and liver in children; improve quality of care by fostering the dissemination of this knowledge through scientific meetings, professional and public education, and policy development; and serve as an effective voice for members and the profession as a whole. Toward these goals, the society organizes meetings, conferences, educational offerings, and committees of pediatric gastroenterologists in the United States. NASPGHAN publications include the peer-reviewed *Journal of Pediatric Gastroenterology and Nutrition* and a quarterly newsletter.

University of Chicago Celiac Disease Center
5841 S. Maryland Ave., Mail Code 4069
Chicago, IL 60637
(773) 702-7593
fax: (773) 702-0666
e-mail: www.cureceliac
disease.org/contact-us
website: www.cure
celiacdisease.org

The University of Chicago Celiac Disease Center is a nonprofit organization founded largely to combat the misconception that celiac disease is a rare disease and to properly educate both the general public and the medical profession. The center consists of a network of doctors who specialize in infertility, thyroid disease, dermatology, diabetes, cancer, and other diseases and disorders that are often associated with celiac disease. These specialists, and other staff at the center, conduct research, raise awareness, and provide education and services to celiac disease patients and the medical community. *Impact* is a quarterly electronic newsletter published by the center that provides information on center events, the latest research, and helpful ideas for living better with celiac disease.

University of Maryland School of Medicine Center for Celiac Research
20 Penn St., Rm. S303B, Baltimore, MD 21201
(410) 706-5516
e-mail: celiaccenter@
peds.umaryland.edu
website: www.celiac
center.org

The University of Maryland Center for Celiac Research is an institution engaged in clinical care, diagnostic support, education, and clinical and basic science research in celiac disease. The goal of the Center for Celiac Research is to increase the awareness of celiac disease in order to provide better care, better quality of life, and more adequate support for the celiac disease community. The center supports cutting-edge, innovative, interactive, multidisciplinary research in all aspects of celiac disease and provides state-of-the-art education opportunities for medical students, graduate students, postdoctoral fellows, and visiting scientists. The center's website provides links to research articles published by center staff, as well as FAQs and other information about celiac disease.

FOR FURTHER READING

Books

Shauna James Ahern, *Gluten-Free Girl*. Hoboken, NJ: John Wiley, 2007.

James Braly, Ron Hoggan, and Jonathan Wright, *Dangerous Grains: Why Gluten Cereal Grains May Be Hazardous to Your Health*. New York: Avery, 2002.

Brett F. Carver, *Wheat: Science and Trade*. Hoboken, NJ: Wiley-Blackwell, 2009.

Melinda Dennis and Daniel Leffler, *Real Life with Celiac Disease*. Bethesda, MD: AGA Press, 2010.

Eimear Gallagher, *Gluten-Free Food Science and Technology*. Hoboken, NJ: John Wiley, 2010.

Peter H.R. Green and Rory Jones, *Celiac Disease: A Hidden Epidemic*. New York: William Morrow, 2010.

Elisabeth Hasselbeck, *The G-Free Diet: A Gluten-Free Survival Guide*. New York: Center Street, 2011.

Kenneth F. Kiple and Kriemhild Coneè Ornelas, *The Cambridge World History of Food*. Cambridge: Cambridge University Press, 2000.

D. Lafiandra, S. Masci, and R. D'Ovidio, *The Gluten Proteins*. Cambridge: Royal Society of Chemistry, 2004.

Jax Peters Lowell and J. DiMarino, *The Gluten-Free Bible*. New York: Holt, 2005.

Adrienne Z. Milligan and William Maltese, *The Gluten-Free Way: My Way*. Rockville, MD: Wildside, 2009.

Vikki Petersen and Richard Petersen, *The Gluten Effect: How "Innocent" Wheat Is Ruining Your Health*. Sunnyvale, CA: True Health, 2009.

Jules E. Dowler Shepard, *The First Year: Celiac Disease and Living Gluten-Free; An Essential Guide for the Newly Diagnosed*. Cambridge, MA: Da Capo, 2008.

Tricia Thompson and Marlisa Brown, *Easy Gluten-Free.* Hoboken, NJ: John Wiley, 2010.

Stephen Wangen, *Healthier Without Wheat: A New Understanding of Wheat Allergies, Celiac Disease, and Non-celiac Gluten Intolerance.* Seattle: Innate Health, 2009.

Periodicals and Internet Sources

William F. Balistreri, "Celiac Disease and Type 1 Diabetes: To Screen or Not to Screen?," *Journal of Pediatrics*, May 2007.

Madonna Behen, "Mouse Study Suggests New Clues to Celiac Disease," *USA Today*, February 12, 2011.

Peter Byass, Kathleen Kahn, and Anneli Ivarsson, "The Global Burden of Childhood Coeliac Disease: A Neglected Component of Diarrhoeal Mortality?," *PLoS One*, July 2011.

Ewen Callaway, "Stone Age Flour Found Across Europe," *Nature*, October 18, 2010.

Sheila Crowe, "Genetic Testing for Celiac Disease," *New York Times*, January 13, 2010.

John Easton, "Human and Mouse Studies Sharpen Focus on Cause of Celiac Disease," *University of Chicago News*, February 15, 2011.

Alessio Fasano, "Surprises from Celiac Disease," *Scientific American*, August 2009.

Alessio Fasano, "Head to Head: Should We Screen for Coeliac Disease? Yes," *British Medical Journal*, September 17, 2009.

Alastair M. Gray and Irene N Papanicolas, "Impact of Symptoms on Quality of Life Before and After Diagnosis of Coeliac Disease," *BMC Health Services Research*, 2010.

Stefano Guandalini, "A Brief History of Celiac Disease," *Impact: University of Chicago Celiac Disease Center Newsletter*, Summer 2007.

Elena Lionetti et al. "Neurology of Childhood Coeliac Disease," *Developmental Medicine & Child Neurology*, August 2010.

Karl Mårild, Anneli Sepa Frostell, and Jonas F Ludvigsson, "Psychological Stress and Coeliac Disease in Childhood: A Cohort Study," *BMC Gastroenterology*, September 14, 2010.

Terri Murphy, "Celiac Disease and the Gluten-Free Diet," Clinical Reference Systems, 2010. www.austinregionalclinic.com /patient_education/mckesson/adult_health_advisor/aha_celiac di_crs.htm.

R. John Presutti, John R. Cangemi, Harvey D. Cassidy, and David A. Hill, "Celiac Disease," *American Family Physician,* December 15, 2007.

Shauna S. Roberts, "Can Thyroid and Celiac Diseases Be Predicted?," *Diabetes Forecast,* July 2006.

Darshak Sanghavi, "Nobody's Normal Anymore," *Slate,* July 22, 2009. www.slate.com/articles/news_and_politics/prescriptions /2009/07/nobodys_normal_anymore.html.

Anne Underwood, "Celiac Disease: The Great Pretender," *Saturday Evening Post,* March/April 2010.

E.F. Verdu, D. Armstrong, and J.A. Murray, "Between Celiac Disease and Irritable Bowel Syndrome: The 'No Man's Land' of Gluten Sensitivity," *American Journal of Gastroenterology,* June 2009.

Chris Woolston, "The Healthy Skeptic: Supplements Claim to Break Down Gluten," *Los Angeles Times,* September 26, 2011.

INDEX